Mastering Lega...

Strategies for Profit, Value, and Innovation

EDITED BY RICHARD BURCHER

Commissioning editor
Alex Davies

Managing director
Sian O'Neill

Mastering Legal Pricing: Strategies for Profit, Value, and Innovation
is published by

Globe Law and Business Ltd
3 Mylor Close
Horsell
Woking
Surrey GU21 4DD
United Kingdom
Tel: +44 20 3745 4770
www.globelawandbusiness.com

Mastering Legal Pricing: Strategies for Profit, Value, and Innovation

ISBN 978-1-83723-091-4
EPUB ISBN 978-1-83723-092-1
Adobe PDF ISBN 978-1-83723-093-8

GPSR Compliance: EU Authorised Representative: Easy Access System Europe - Mustamäe tee 50, 10621 Tallinn, Estonia, gpsr.requests@easproject.com

DISCLAIMER
This publication is intended as a general guide only. The information and opinions which it contains are not intended to be a comprehensive study, or to provide legal advice, and should not be treated as a substitute for legal advice concerning particular situations. Legal advice should always be sought before taking any action based on the information provided. The publisher bears no responsibility for any errors or omissions contained herein.

Contents

Executive summary

The legal profession is undergoing a significant transformation in how its services are priced. The traditional billable hour model, which has dominated for decades, is increasingly being questioned by clients, firms, and legal professionals alike. The world of legal pricing is evolving rapidly, driven by shifts in client expectations, technological advancements, and new market dynamics. Law firms and legal professionals must adapt to these changes to stay competitive, ensure profitability, and meet the demands of a diverse and increasingly cost-conscious client base.

This book explores the evolving landscape of legal pricing, addressing the challenges and opportunities that law firms face in adapting to modern economic demands. From the traditional billable hour to alternative models such as subscription-based services and value-based pricing, our contributors examine the impact of client expectations, technology, and evolving business strategies. The chapters that follow provide insight into the tools, frameworks, and strategies necessary to create more transparent and efficient pricing models that align with both client needs and law firm profitability.

Our opening chapter, by Michael Roster, looks at the changing landscape of legal pricing and provides an introduction to what will follow. Michael asks readers to consider the ideas proposed throughout the book and then examine how best to implement the changes – changes that many if not most think are inevitable.

Chapter two, by James G. Perkins and Tiffany O'Neil, provides a comprehensive look at the changing economics of legal service delivery, tracing the industry's gradual movement away from the billable hour and toward models that emphasize client-centered value and predictability. They begin by exploring the historical decline in billable hour dominance – supported by Procopio's internal data since 2012 – and examine the forces prompting this shift, including client pressure, competitive differentiation, and technology-enabled alternatives.

The discussion then turns to the rise of alternative pricing strategies such as fixed fees, subscriptions, and value-based models, and how these models are being received by clients and the legal profession alike.

A key focus is placed on the authors' own operational pivot toward fixed-fee arrangements, highlighting how this strategy aligns with modern client expectations around cost certainty. Through their initiative with Legal Six Sigma, they illustrate how data-driven process improvement, standardization, and internal change management have enabled them to roll out fixed-fee pricing across multiple legal practice areas. James and Tiffany share practical guidance on how firms can implement these models effectively without sacrificing quality or profitability. Ultimately, the chapter interrogates whether the legal industry is undergoing a true pricing transformation or merely adapting old norms to new expectations – and what that means for the future of legal service delivery.

Stéphanie Hamon then follows this up in chapter 3, explaining why aligning client expectations with perceived value is essential to building trust, ensuring satisfaction, and maintaining long-term relationships. Legal service providers must move beyond traditional billing models and embrace approaches that prioritize outcomes, transparency, and collaboration.

Value is matter-specific. What one client values – speed, certainty, innovation – may differ entirely from another's priorities. This variability makes robust matter scoping indispensable. Effective scoping sets the foundation for accurate pricing, fosters mutual accountability, and reduces the risk of misalignment. Historically, the billable hour has dominated legal pricing, but its limitations have become apparent. The shift toward Alternative Fee Arrangements (AFAs) and Effective Fee Arrangements (EFAs) reflects a movement toward pricing models aligned with client-defined value. EFAs – such as fixed fees, milestone pricing, retainers, and gainshare models – enable clients to control costs while incentivizing legal providers to deliver results.

Managing expectations requires continuous, two-way communication throughout the matter lifecycle. Legal providers must proactively communicate budget updates, flag risks early, and be transparent about deviations from the plan. Clients must articulate their evolving needs and provide timely feedback. This ongoing exchange is critical to preventing surprises and ensuring alignment. Ultimately, aligning expectations with value perception requires a cultural shift. Legal providers must move from billing hours to delivering impact. Clients must engage in open and ongoing communication. When both sides embrace this partnership model, pricing becomes a strategic enabler of trust, efficiency, and shared success.

Chapter 4 by Steven A. Lauer explores the concept of "value-related qualities" (or VRQs), which are useful to think about in terms of the ways that legal service can be addressed. They can be used to develop alternative fee arrangements, to develop and manage project plans for lawyers' efforts and to restructure the relationship between inside and outside counsel.

Chapter 5, by Tanbir Jasimuddin, looks at the role of data and analytics in modern legal pricing. We are in an era shaped by the most profound transformation in how legal services are priced and valued. This is driven by client demands for transparency and predictability, and the emerging power and accessibility of data analytics and artificial intelligence. As a result, clients are demanding a move away from the traditional billable hour model to more sophisticated, data-informed approaches. In this chapter, Tanbir examines how law firms can combine historical data, performance metrics, and client intelligence to build their pricing strategies. He discusses how AI can enhance pricing accuracy, predicting costs and automating tasks and workflows. Additionally, the chapter outlines implementation challenges, including data governance and change management. Getting this right will ultimately deliver increased profitability and client satisfaction.

Chapter 6 by the book's consulting editor, Richard Burcher, looks at behavioral economics in legal pricing, and how to understand client psychology. Richard explores the critical role of behavioral economics in shaping more effective, client-centered legal pricing strategies. As law firms move away from rigid, input-based billing and toward models that reflect value and outcomes, understanding how clients *perceive* price becomes as important as how firms *calculate* it.

At its core, behavioral economics reveals that clients are not perfectly rational actors. Their pricing decisions are shaped by cognitive biases, emotional responses, and contextual cues. Principles such as anchoring, framing, loss aversion, choice architecture, and social proof are not abstract theories – they are powerful levers that directly influence how legal fees are received, evaluated, and acted upon. The chapter begins by challenging the assumption that pricing is a neutral, mathematical exchange. In truth, pricing is a form of communication – one that signals competence, confidence, and value. The way a fee is presented can determine whether it is perceived as reasonable or excessive, transparent or opaque, bespoke or generic.

Through practical illustrations, the chapter demonstrates how anchoring a proposal against a higher benchmark or framing an offer as a gain rather than a cost, can significantly shift client reactions. It also examines the decoy effect – where presenting a third, less attractive option can make a target fee appear more palatable – and the power of tiered pricing structures, which give clients a sense of control and comparative value. Importantly, behavioral economics also offers insight into the emotional dimensions of legal pricing. Clients seek not only value for money but also fairness, predictability, and reassurance. The chapter explores how law firms can use transparent scoping, menu pricing, and confidence-based guarantees to reduce anxiety and build trust – particularly in high-stakes or emotionally charged matters.

Another key theme is the role of perceived effort versus perceived expertise. Clients often conflate time spent with value delivered, unless the firm actively educates them otherwise. Behavioral science can help reframe this dynamic, positioning legal fees in terms of risk mitigation, strategic insight, or long-term savings, rather than effort alone. The chapter also addresses internal applications of behavioral economics. How partners price, discount, and communicate value is often shaped by their own biases – such as loss aversion (fear of losing the client) or anchoring to last year's fee. Firms that build behavioral awareness into their pricing training and governance structures will be better equipped to price confidently, consistently, and commercially.

In closing, the chapter argues that behavioral economics is not just a tactical toolkit – it is a strategic mindset. It equips firms to move beyond transactional pricing and engage in pricing conversations that are empathetic, persuasive, and client aligned. In an increasingly sophisticated market, where clients evaluate not just what they pay but *how* they are made to feel about it, mastering the psychology of pricing will be a key differentiator.

In today's legal market, clients continue to demand more transparency in their legal engagements. Gone are the days when clients were loyal to just one firm – thus, they continue to shop for the most competitive price on legal services. As a result, firms must be transparent about scoping and put more emphasis on the value they bring to the market. They need to be ready to adapt to new strategies like AFAs and fixed fee engagements to mitigate write-offs and write-downs that undermine profitability. By leveraging the proper people, processes, and technologies, firms are able to increase communication and even educate their clients on how to be savvy while they pursue legal engagements, so the firm can attain its desired rates and realization. In chapter 7, Jack Kingston discusses how pricing departments can leverage relationships and transparency to remain profitable in the ever-changing market. It also addresses how technology and advanced processes can enable law firms to enhance communication with their clients, leading to increased customer satisfaction.

Richard Burcher then returns in chapter 8 to discuss fixed fees and predictability, and how these help meet modern client demands.

In chapter 9, Tim Corcoran explores how traditional law firm partner compensation models often undermine profitability and innovation due to misaligned incentives. He opens with an analogy from retail, illustrating how short-term revenue-focused decisions – like discounting without regard to profit – can lead to long-term business failure. Similarly, law firms often prioritize revenue through billable hours and origination credits, while ignoring more strategic metrics such as profitability, leverage, and client value.

Tim introduces the R.U.L.E.S. framework – Realization, Utilization, Leverage, Expenses, and Speed of collections – to explain how these factors affect a firm's financial health. Many compensation systems, however, incentivize partners to hoard work, underprice services, or pursue billing volume at the expense of profit margins and client relationships. This is exacerbated when firms focus internally rather than considering market value and external benchmarks, leading to distorted perceptions of partner contributions based solely on billing rates. He critiques outdated "cost-plus" pricing and tenure-based rate models, arguing they ignore client-perceived value and market conditions. Case studies highlight how innovation efforts, such as workflow automation, often fail to yield intended profit gains when partner compensation punishes efficiency by reducing billable hours.

Tim challenges firms to reassess whether partners are treated as high-paid employees or as true business owners. He advocates for rewarding behaviors that enhance long-term firm value – like delegation, innovation, and client loyalty – over individual billing achievements. Adjusting compensation plans is politically difficult, but essential for firms seeking to thrive in a competitive, client-driven market. Ultimately, the chapter urges law firm leaders to shift from tradition-bound, revenue-centric models to incentive systems that align partner behavior with sustainable profitability, client satisfaction, and firm-wide success.

In Chapter 10, Benjamin Viney addresses some of the challenges associated with partner and associate compensation in law firms. He explores the psychology of pay and value, the ways in which firms compensate different types of contribution (including the thorny question of leadership compensation), and how this has changed over the last 40 years. He also looks at the implications of a potential decline of the billable hour on compensation models, and the importance of the EU Pay Transparency Directive.

Richard Burcher returns in chapter 11 to discuss the intersection of technology and legal pricing. His chapter explores the profound dual impact of technology – particularly artificial intelligence (AI) – on the pricing of legal services. He argues that AI is not merely enhancing legal pricing practice, it is fundamentally reshaping both *how* firms price and *what* they are pricing.

The first dimension of this transformation is the use of AI within the pricing process itself. Here, technology serves as an enabler of unprecedented capability. AI-driven pricing tools support matter profiling, scenario modelling, profitability forecasting, and real-time budgeting.

These capabilities empower pricing professionals and lawyers alike to construct more accurate, competitive, and client-aligned fee proposals. Pricing becomes less reactive and more predictive – rooted in data, benchmarks, and behavioral insights. This gives rise to what the chapter terms "pricing enablement infrastructure" – a fusion of intelligent software, internal governance, and commercial capability that supports law firms in designing and defending complex pricing models.

The second and equally disruptive dimension is the impact of hybrid AI/human service delivery on pricing architecture. As law firms increasingly combine machine-driven tasks (e.g. contract review, document drafting, risk flagging) with human legal advisory, they face a fundamental challenge – how to price a service that is no longer purely based on human time and effort.

Traditional metrics – such as hourly rates or time estimates – are insufficient. Instead, firms must adopt new value narratives that recognize the interplay of machine efficiency, human judgment, and client-perceived value. This hybrid model necessitates alternative pricing constructs – fixed fees, modular pricing, success fees, and subscription arrangements – that reflect outcome orientation and service deconstruction. Crucially, the chapter argues that this is not a future trend but a present strategic imperative. Clients are already expecting pricing transparency, technological leverage, and commercially progressive options. Firms that cannot articulate how technology influences both their service delivery and their pricing risk appearing outdated or opaque.

In closing, Richard calls for a reimagining of pricing as a core discipline – blending commercial acuity, behavioral economics, technological literacy, and strategic storytelling. Those who lead this transition will gain not just pricing sophistication, but competitive advantage in an increasingly commoditized and client-driven legal market.

Navigating legal procurement has become a defining feature of how law firms win and retain work. Once confined largely to the public sector, structured procurement processes are now widespread in private practice, driven by in-house procurement teams, legal operations, and specialist agencies. For legal pricing professionals, procurement presents both challenges and opportunities – it shapes client expectations, influences pricing strategies, and tests the profitability of engagements. Chapter 12 by Steph Hogg explores how to navigate legal procurement effectively. It examines common pitfalls, offers a structured framework for assessing and responding to tenders, and highlights practical approaches to pricing, negotiation, and relationship management. By understanding procurement's objectives and aligning responses with client value, pricing professionals can improve tender success, protect sustainable margins, and position their firms for long-term competitive advantage.

Tanbir Jasimuddin returns in chapter 13 to discuss how we can measure success in terms of metrics and KPIs for legal pricing models. How can firms evaluate whether their pricing strategies are truly effective in terms of both client satisfaction and profitability?

In chapter 14 Richard Burcher concludes the book with a look at the future of legal pricing. This final chapter provides a five-year forecast of legal pricing, positioning it as a strategic capability at the center of law firm competitiveness and client value. As pricing evolves from an administrative function to a sophisticated commercial discipline, firms must adapt across three critical dimensions – technology, client engagement, and internal capability.

Technology's dual impact is reshaping both the mechanics of pricing and the nature of legal service delivery. On one front, AI-powered platforms enable smarter pricing – through data-driven modelling, profitability forecasting, and scenario analysis. On the other, the rise of hybrid AI/human service delivery is redefining what's being priced. Law firms must now account for a blend of automation and legal expertise, shifting focus from time spent to value delivered. The decline of hourly billing is accelerating – not through abolition, but through marginalization. Its misalignment with client expectations around efficiency, transparency, and risk-sharing has catalyzed demand for value-based pricing. Aligning fees with client-defined outcomes and strategic importance, this model rewards collaboration, results, and trust.

A key theme is the professionalization of legal pricing within firms. Pricing professionals are no longer back-office analysts – they are now strategic partners, embedded in client teams, guiding fee design, negotiations, and commercial planning. Their expertise spans behavioral economics, data interpretation, and stakeholder engagement, making them essential to modern legal practice.

Firms are introducing formal governance structures – pricing committees, deal desks, and approval workflows – while evolving partner incentives to reward pricing discipline and margin performance. Behavioral pricing techniques such as anchoring, bundling, and tiered options are becoming mainstream, supported by AI-generated fee narratives and guided scoping tools that facilitate better client conversations. The chapter also examines emerging pricing models such as subscriptions, outcome-based fees, and success arrangements. These are not simply innovations but responses to rising client expectations for predictability, partnership, and measurable value. They also offer firms opportunities to expand access to justice and scale delivery models sustainably.

Ultimately, pricing will be a defining capability for the next generation of law firms. Those that embed pricing into their strategic, technological, and cultural fabric – led by empowered professionals and enabled by intelligent infrastructure – will lead the market. Those that do not will be left behind.

About the editor

Richard Burcher, founder and managing director of Validatum®, and founder and CEO of Virtual Pricing Director®, is a globally recognized authority on legal services pricing. A former practicing lawyer and managing partner in New Zealand, he has over 45 years' experience in the legal sector. Following postgraduate study in pricing science and behavioral economics, he established Validatum® as a leading consultancy in legal pricing, now having worked with over 300 firms in 30 countries, including 43 of the UK Top 100.

A prolific educator, Richard is a senior teaching fellow at the Australian College of Law and a fellow of the US College of Law Practice Management. He holds ALPP Platinum Plus accreditation from the True Value Partnering Institute and was named Pricing Educator of the Year in 2025.

In 2023, Richard launched Virtual Pricing Director®, a cloud-based legal pricing, profitability, and matter management platform, now being adopted globally and included in elite incubators such as Slaughter and May's Collaborate and A&O Shearman's Fuse. He has advised firms ranging from £10m to £3bn turnover on pricing strategy, governance, analytics, and education.

Widely published and cited, Richard's thought leadership shapes pricing practices across the legal industry, underpinned by his belief in a holistic "people, process, and technology" approach.

About the authors

Tim Corcoran is a former CEO who now guides law firm and law department leaders through the profitable disruption of outdated business models. Tim is a trustee and fellow of the College of Law Practice Management, former president of the Legal Marketing Association and a member of its Hall of Fame, an American Lawyer Research fellow, a past teaching fellow in the Master in Legal Business program at the Australian College of Law, a frequent presenter at lawyer retreats and legal conferences, and a writer whose articles are published regularly in leading publications. This is the tenth chapter Tim has contributed to a Globe Law and Business publication.

Stéphanie Hamon is helping legal functions to operate as an efficient business partner. She is changing legal service delivery, one step at a time and an expert in setting and delivering transformation programs and commercial management strategies for in-house legal departments, as well as broader legal operations strategies and implementation. She led the Barclays team that was named "Legal operations team of the year" at the 2019 UK Legal 500 Awards. She has also developed a new approach to law firm panels and engagement with the broader legal ecosystem. She promotes collaboration, relationship, and efficiencies. She has over 20 years' experience working with legal and financial institutions in the UK, Europe, and Asia Pacific. Stéphanie has considerable expertise in senior stakeholder management, business development, strategy formulation and execution, and client-focused relationship management. Most recently she founded a first-of-its-kind legal operations consulting practice at Norton Rose where she was recognized with an individual Band 1 ranking in Chambers. Clients have said about her: "Stéphanie Hamon's one of the best in the business. I appreciate that she is not afraid to give tough advice or push back." "Stéphanie is one of the top change leaders and collaborators in our sector." Stéphanie has now rejoined the in-house side, working as global head of legal external engagement at HSBC.

Steph Hogg is director of procurement consulting at Validatum. She is a seasoned procurement professional with over 15 years' experience gained in the financial services sector as head of legal procurement for a FTSE 100 insurance company, and is one of only a handful of legal procurement specialists in the UK regularly working with the largest and most sophisticated of law firms. Bringing thought leadership to the sector, she has unrivalled practical experience in running legal panel processes and developing and maintaining successful, collaborative relationships, underpinned by world class MI and reporting that truly meets client needs. Respected by legal firms for being honest and straight talking, Steph is passionate about helping firms and their clients work together to define and deliver excellent value for money, and is very clear on the difference between value and price! A regular conference speaker and author on legal procurement, Steph's unique insights also draw upon first-hand experience gained in commodities as diverse as IT and consultancy, and make her uniquely placed to help firms navigate the professional, institutionalized approach to buying now endemic within the legal profession. Steph works exclusively with law firms to help them optimize external legal procurement relationships.

Tanbir Jasimuddin is an award-winning finance and transformation leader with 20 years' experience within legal and professional services. He is an ex-McKinsey and Big Four management consultant and has also held finance leadership positions at several law firms. He has a track record of delivering performance improvement across organizations. Tanbir has a passion for using data and analytics for driving behaviors. He is a recognized expert in finance and analytics and has authored several papers on these topics.

Jack Kingston has spent over 20 years in the legal technology industry, driven by a passion for helping law firms boost profitability and achieve operational excellence through the strategic use of process and technology. Guided by his personal "why", which is to consistently thrive while building lasting relationships with loyal and ambitious people, Jack brings both vision and integrity to every partnership. Outside of work, he enjoys alpine skiing, spending time with friends, and following baseball. He has also dedicated 27 years as a Canadian football referee, demonstrating his commitment to leadership, discipline, and community involvement.

Steven A. Lauer consults with corporate law departments and law firms on the value of legal service and related topics. For several years, he consulted with corporate law departments and law firms on issues related to how in-house and outside counsel work together. He spent over 15 years as an in-house attorney in law departments ranging in size from one to 400 lawyers, in the real estate and compliance industries, and over two years as executive vice president, deputy editor and publisher of *The Metropolitan Corporate Counsel*, a monthly journal for in-house attorneys. Steve conducts benchmarking research for clients, designs evaluation processes for counsel selection, and researches and designs case-evaluation methodologies that incorporate clients' appetites for risk and goals, among other projects. He has consulted on alternative fee arrangements, task-based billing, and client expectations. He has written numerous articles on compliance, the relations between in-house and outside attorneys, the selection of counsel by corporate clients, the evaluation of legal service, litigation management, and other topics relevant to corporate compliance programs and corporate legal service and has organized and spoken at numerous conferences in respect of those subjects.

Tiffany O'Neil is director of KM and technology innovation at Procopio, Cory, Hargreaves and Savitch LLP. For 15+ years, Tiffany has led Procopio's knowledge management (KM) and records/office services functions, and since 2019 has also presided over the firm's technology innovation group. With more than 25 years of KM and research expertise, she oversees investigative, business, and legal research; evaluates and implements KM tools and processes; and develops strategies to enhance workflow efficiency across legal and administrative departments. Tiffany trains attorneys and staff in effective research techniques and drives adoption of innovative solutions that advance operational performance. She is also an active member of the Procopio Enterprise Risk Management Committee. Before joining Procopio, Tiffany worked at various law firms and served as an information specialist at McKinsey & Company, a global management consulting leader.

James (Jim) G. Perkins is chief operating officer and chief compliance officer at Procopio, Cory, Hargreaves and Savitch LLP. For the last 25+ years, Jim has led Procopio's non-legal operations including finance, human resources, administration, marketing and business development, information services, and knowledge management. He is a member of the firm's management committee and in 2012 also became the firm's CCO, responsible for developing a firm Enterprise Risk Management Program. In his CCO capacity he also serves as co-chair, together with the firm's general counsel, of Procopio's Enterprise Risk Management Committee. Over the years, Jim has spoken regularly on law firm management issues and business strategy at conferences and international law firm network meetings, in addition to authoring several articles on the role of COOs in law firms, law firm profitability, and technology. He also consults occasionally as part of the Procopio Business Advisors affiliate. Prior to joining Procopio, Jim served in various leadership capacities at professional service firms in both the US and UK. He has a PhD from the University of Surrey, England, and an MBA from the University of Chicago.

Michael Roster was formerly managing partner of Morrison & Foerster's Los Angeles office, co-chair of the firm's Financial Institutions Practice Group worldwide, resident in both LA and DC, and a member of the firm's policy committee. In 1993, Mike was appointed general counsel of Stanford University, Stanford Medical Center, and Stanford Management Company. He subsequently was executive vice president and general counsel of Golden West Financial Corporation. Mike has served as chair of the Association of Corporate Counsel (currently 45,000 in-house lawyer members worldwide), chair of the Stanford Alumni Association, steering committee co-chair of ACC's Value Challenge, and chair of two start-up companies. Mike currently teaches Contract Drafting and Analysis at the University of Southern California's Gould School of Law and is also currently a director of MDRC in New York, a non-profit organization that evaluates the effectiveness of government and other programs affecting lower income families and individuals.

Benjamin Viney is WTW's practice lead for work, rewards, and careers, GB and Ireland. He advises clients on partner and associate pay, performance and related areas, and specializes in working with global professional services firms, including legal, accounting, consulting, engineering, surveying, architects, and executive search. Benjamin has undertaken extensive research on partner pay and performance, highlighting key trends in partner compensation.

Chapter 1:
The changing landscape of legal pricing

By Michael Roster

Kodak. Motorola. Sears. Blockbuster. I have long mentioned these companies (and others) when discussing pricing issues with both law firm leaders and corporate counsel. It usually takes them a few seconds to realize that all of these are companies that incurred significant losses and often have failed. But I point out there's a still more important story about these companies, in that every one of them once held a majority of market share in their respective industries, and several of them actually failed within one or two years after they were the market leaders.

My message is simple – if everything is going well for your law firm or law department, why in the world would you change? Even if you wanted to introduce change, there are major forces working against you – your organization's culture, all the support systems that measure efficiencies and billings, and the fact that most people – lawyers especially – hate change. It thus is often the upstart that isn't burdened with the history of success that makes the breakthroughs and eventually replaces former market leaders.

Pricing legal services has always been a challenge, although I think back on the most successful firms that I used as a general counsel and their pricing was "whatever you think it was worth".

As some readers may know, when I was at Morrison & Foerster, our then-chair had decided we should move the entire firm off billable hours and back to fixed pricing. Among other things, our chair noted that we had been using billable hours for only the past 15 to 20 years. Prior to that, our fees were at fixed prices, retainers, and contingency arrangements and the firm was extremely successful with these methods – not only in profitability but in creating a professional environment where partners and associates loved to practice law.

I also remember when realization rates (that is, the percent actually paid by clients as compared to the hours that had been logged for matters and firmwide) were around 93 to 95 percent. In subsequent years, when some colleagues and I headed the Association of Corporate Counsel's Value Challenge (that is, an attempt to get law firms and in-house counsel to focus again on value), I met confidentially with numerous law firm management committees and was surprised to learn that many of their realization rates were now in the low 80 percent range, and in one meeting, the partners learned for the first time that their firm had descended into the upper 70 percent range.

But here's what should be most important to law firm leaders as they navigate the accelerating changes in our profession. When they go back to fixed and similar value pricing initiatives, and especially with a focused use of AI combined with fixed pricing, retainers, and similar arrangements, their realization rates should actually exceed 100 percent.

In the process, it is critical that in-house counsel and their procurement specialists not ask to see shadow hours – that is, hours devoted to a given matter as compared to what is billed. Hours should go back to being nothing more than an internal measure, seen only by law firm managers, of where lawyer time is being deployed but definitely not determinative of the value of the matter itself. Likewise, if you look at the New York formula for setting billing rates, one-third is for associate and related compensation, one-third is for overhead, and one-third is for firm profitability. It was foolish from the outset for law firms to stake their profitability on hours spent when profitability should be based on expertise, efficiency, and the quality of the product that is produced.

After my first year as general counsel at Stanford, we reduced the number of in-house lawyers and paralegals from 27 to seven and outsourced our legal work to three law firms (eventually five) with fixed prices per portfolio. Pricing for the HR/labor portfolio was based on what we had been spending on such matters, on average, over the prior five or so years. The portfolio included both counseling and litigation (with predetermined carveouts) on the theory that once firms were again rewarded for applying expertise to our matters, not hours, not only could the firms achieve better outcomes but in fact we would have fewer legal problems over time. And that turned out to be the case. At the end of the first year, our total legal costs (both in-house and outside counsel combined) had declined by 20 percent and, if we had pushed the reforms harder, might have been reduced by 25 percent and as much as 33 percent. (Virtually every other company that engaged in a similar reorganization process came to the exact same percentages.) At the end of five years, we had half the litigation we had had the prior decade.

Many law firm and in-house lawyers say it's not possible to predict the cost of matters given the vagaries of the regulatory agencies, the courts, the plaintiffs and their counsel and the like. That might be true, matter for matter. But if law firm and in-house lawyers look at their entire portfolios of specific types of matters (labor, securities, environmental, tax, IT, etc.), they will see that the matters, as a group, follow a highly predictable pattern. Some individual matters go a bit higher and some go a bit lower, and occasionally there will be an extraordinary matter that goes out of bounds. But the number of such extraordinary matters is usually quite rare, and of course they need to be handled differently. Otherwise, the matters follow a very predictable pattern, so now the task is to try to reduce the cost of that pattern while improving outcomes, and rewarding both law firm and in-house lawyers for reducing costs while improving outcomes.

The authors of the various chapters that follow discuss some critically important issues about pricing and related issues. What the authors discuss is a return to basics. The challenge for law firm and in-house lawyers is to consider what is proposed throughout this book and then see how best to implement the changes – changes, by the way, that many if not most of us think are inevitable.

Most of my general counsel colleagues found that, when they tried to revamp how legal work was handled, they lost approximately a third of their in-house lawyers. We all initially tried to convince our existing lawyers of the benefits of what was being done but eventually realized that most of the hold-outs weren't going to change and some were even going to undermine the transition. It was best to help those lawyers who didn't want to change to move on.

Law firm leaders may find a similar resistance to change, although it will be best to start with practice groups that welcome the changes and to give them the necessary support for the transitions. Those success stories can then be used with other practice groups. And frankly, there are some practice groups that probably shouldn't change. At one law firm I met with, the firm had massive dominance in a specific type of matter and billed at premium rates. In those cases, I told the firm's leaders, stick with what was working but at the same time, gain experience with alternatives so that if and when a specific client asked if the work could be priced on a different basis, the answer would be, "Of course it can be, in fact we've got lots of experience with these types of alternatives". And along the way, hopefully the practice group's leaders would be highly confident about how to do the work on a different basis and might even know, if done right, the work might be even more profitable even as the firm meets and exceeds client expectations.

In summary, the task for readers is first to grasp what is being proposed, but then comes the harder part – how do you get from here to there?

Chapter 2:
Rethinking legal pricing – from billable hours to value and profitability

By James G. Perkins, Ph.D., chief operating officer and chief compliance officer, and Tiffany M. O'Neil, J.D., director of KM and technology innovation, Procopio, Cory, Hargreaves and Savitch LLP

Death of the billable hour – maybe?

Generative AI (genAI) is redefining the way law firms produce work and manage efficiency. Prior to the explosion of genAI, firms relied on traditional automation to handle repetitive processes, but genAI has revolutionized workflows – not only undertaking tasks faster but working in a way that is context-aware, adaptive, and capable of producing human-quality outputs. In addition to potential time savings, there is a transformative shift in where lawyers focus their energy. This affects how clients experience services, increases efficiencies, and the way law firms add value.

The birth of many serious genAI products into the legal industry has once again brought to the fore the issue of the decline of billable hours, similar to the cries that followed the recessionary periods after the dot.com explosion in 1998-2000 and the financial crisis in 2007-2009. However, this time there does seem to be more potential. As detailed by Ethan Batraski,[1] the legal industry represents one of the last great market inefficiencies in the modern economy. We have trained clients to equate hours worked and billed with value delivered, creating the only major industry where productivity gains threaten profitability. It should be noted that over the last five years, surveys show that although demand (gross billable hours) in US law firms has only grown by, on average, 1.6 percent each year (with productivity staying the same, at best), overall revenue and profits per partner have increased by eight to nine percent and nine to ten percent per year respectively, because of the billable hour model and rates that have increased by about seven percent annually. Without the billable hours model being alive and well, the revenue increases would not have been so significant.

And it's not just in the last five years – in the last two decades, almost every survey shows that billable hour-driven revenue increases have predominately come from increases in billing rates. Is the gravy train ending? Baranski believes there will be significant cost savings (50 percent+) in output-based pricing using genAI+ legal products. At present, the market does not have enough experience to validate such numbers. However, there is no doubt in our minds, based on preliminary work in the last year, that serious savings can be obtained.

At Procopio, we have tracked in detail our alternative fee agreement (AFA) matters and revenue since 2012. Figure 1 shows that, after the financial crisis of 2008-10, we had an average percentage of AFA matters of about 15-25 percent and from 2018 we have averaged about 35-40 percent, primarily because of the increase in IP fixed fee work. Regular billable hours work has been consistent for the last few years at around 60 percent of total matters. Overall revenue from AFAs has accounted for around 15 percent of the total, with about 85 percent of revenue coming from regular billable hours work. We suspect these percentages are probably not far off the norm for other mid-size firms, so we can see that we are all still very vulnerable financially to billable hours being significantly decreased due to AI.

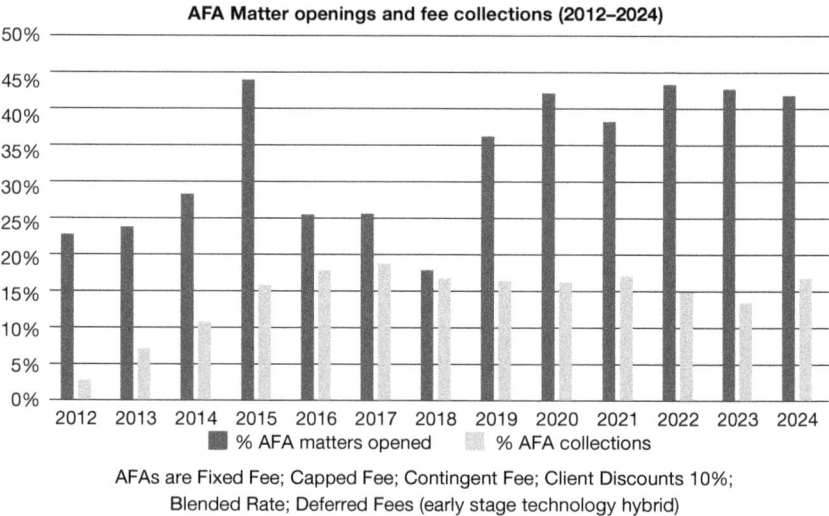

AFA Matter openings and fee collections (2012–2024)

AFAs are Fixed Fee; Capped Fee; Contingent Fee; Client Discounts 10%;
Blended Rate; Deferred Fees (early stage technology hybrid)

Figure 1: Alternative fee agreement (AFA) matters and revenue.
Source: Procopio.

In terms of our AI experience at Procopio, we have seen 20-30 percent savings on fixed fee AFA patent work using two specific IP genAI products, thus allowing us, at this time, to improve our margins substantially. In other practice areas it is very much a task-by-task, project-by-project analysis, but we do see 10-30 percent worked time decreases with some projects.

Baranski talks about the market perception shift that is happening now – from the "Old World" approach of "We pay for the time of the best lawyers" to the "New World" approach of "We pay for guaranteed results at a predictable price". Some interpret this as billable hours now becoming a liability, but we should remind ourselves that when we move from the Old World to the New (note it is not if, but when), we still need to "track" our billable hours – in fact track them with even more accuracy than today. When value/outcome-based pricing starts to take hold, firms will need to understand that for accurate costing they need to track every hour worked on the specific project/matter. They will need to understand cost-accounting profitability[2] and develop sensible business models, just as other professional service firms have done for many years.

Law firms capture terabytes of data, they always have. However, the data was never initially input in a seriously organized manner, concentrating forever on just billable hours, fee collections, originations credits – the key factors we needed to bill our clients and pay our attorneys. We never entered detailed matter descriptions in formats that could easily be searched to make sense. Our "experience" history has never been easy for us to extract and many of us are now at a serious disadvantage when we try and match matter experience to pricing. Accounting firms, management consulting firms, and other professions that track their time so as to bill their project fixed fees have been matching their specific projects to accurate costs for years and so have an accurate data set for project costing. Law firms, with their obsession with revenue, have neglected that same level of accuracy. Thus, as the industry moves more to value pricing, this lack of detailed cost data will impede our progress to being as profitable as we should be. We expect that genAI will allow us to mine our own data a lot better than in the past to help us in this endeavor.

So, will the present economic uncertainty and volatility, combined with the rapid advance of the introduction of AI products, eventually break the 25-year steady advance of rate increases in the legal industry? Mark Medice[3] states that in a recent survey, 80 percent of respondents report no significantly productivity gains from the use of AI. In addition, 60 percent say that their pricing approach has not changed due to AI, although 40 percent are beginning to adapt or plan to do so. It is too early for anyone to state exactly how the billable hour model will change because of the products today and future genAI developments, but it will change. To quote our good colleague Ralph Baxter, "The way law is practiced today is completely different from how it will be practiced in ten years, and that change will come as a result of generative AI".[4]

AI in action

While artificial intelligence has been around for decades, the genAI that we know today has already shown that significant progress is possible as it has continued to evolve at a rapid pace. Tools that imported client matter information from forms, tracked renewals, generated reports, or created standardized document packets have started to cut administrative work from, in some cases, days to hours. Processes that once required staff to manage spreadsheets, calendars, and emails have become more streamlined, with automated reminders and escalation notices. These improvements will start to remove much of the clerical burden and automation will scale efficiency and reduce risk when applied to structured, rule-based workflows. Unlike traditional automation, which follows defined rules, genAI can interpret nuance, generate language, and adapt to context. That means it can step into work that used to require hours completing mundane tasks. The impact is beginning to be seen across several areas of practice.

Contract review is one example. Previously, attorneys spent hours combing through various clauses, liability caps, and termination terms. With genAI, firms can generate first-draft redlines automatically. What once required multiple layers of review can now be completed in a fraction of the time, reducing first-pass review by as much as half. Attorneys still apply their judgment, but they are starting from a higher-quality draft and can focus on the nuances rather than the obvious issues. The use of genAI is not the finish line, and probably never will be, but it is often an excellent starting point.

Intellectual property operations provide another strong example. Historically, staff tracked renewal deadlines with manual reminders and spreadsheets, monitoring notices from regulators and contacting clients accordingly. Automation simplifies much of that administrative work. Adding genAI on top transforms the communication itself. Instead of sending a generic notice, the system can explain why a deadline matters, what risks the client faces if it is missed, and what strategies might be used to manage costs. This shifts the value of the communication from being purely transactional to being advisory. In the IP patent area, we have already observed a 20-40 percent reduction in time to complete the task satisfactorily, doubling profit margins.

On the administrative side, billing and reporting are already benefiting from genAI, either via third-party products or embedded genAI in the major legal administrative systems used.

Where once billing cycles lagged because of reconciliation delays and inconsistent narrative drafting, genAI can now generate billing entries that are narrative-ready, enforce consistency across timekeepers, and flag vague or non-compliant descriptions. This has the potential to shorten billing cycles, reduce the risk of client pushback, and improve transparency. Client communication can also benefit from genAI. Memos filled with legal jargon often go unread by busy executives. With genAI, those same memos can be reframed into clear, concise executive summaries, technical guidance for engineers, or practical FAQs for HR leaders. Our firm has had many successes in using genAI to rewrite complex legal documents into user-friendly language and the attorney no longer needs to rewrite themselves; they only need to review for accuracy.

GenAI has become an accelerator in our daily workflows. By acquiring OpenAI's ChatGPT Enterprise platform, Procopio can now tailor ChatGPT (called internally the P-ChatGPT Platform) to our specific legal and business needs while maintaining the required level of security and confidentiality around client data. We have created customized GPTs – single- purpose chatbots configured within the P-ChatGPT framework using tailored instructions and data to perform targeted tasks. These proofs of concept operate within the P-ChatGPT interface and can be replicated or extended via the OpenAI API to integrate with other systems, applications, and custom development.

An administrative example is where we took a manual process that was required to extract information received from clients, organize the data, and perform verification through the USPTO. This task consumed approximately 80 percent of a full-time employee's weekly capacity. We customized our internal P-ChatGPT platform to automatically take the pdfs received from the client, capture the essential details, and confirm those details with the USPTO using an API. What historically took a staff member approximately 30 hours per week is now reduced to two hours per week, with cost savings of about $100,000 per year. We also created a tool for trademark renewals. This genAI tool analyzes and submits specimens for a trademark application or renewal and evaluates their suitability, quality, and robustness based on USPTO guidelines. It connects to the USPTO API to check previously submitted specimens and compares them to bolster feedback.

We are also engaging in reviews of the third-party genAI-driven start-up tools that are now becoming available. The goal is to leverage specialized platforms to deliver faster, better results in specific, niche practice areas, including:

- Due diligence review for M&A transactions.
- Patent and office action response drafting, as well as patent claim chart generation, prior art searching and invalidity searching.
- Trusts and estate forms.

The lessons from all these deployments are clear. Human oversight remains essential.

GenAI can draft and analyze, but professionals must guide judgment, ensure accuracy, and supervise work by all junior attorneys, just as in the past. Data quality is another critical factor. Poor inputs will yield poor outputs, so as indicated above clean data and well-structured knowledge bases are vital. Efficiency should not be mistaken for cost-cutting alone. The true value lies in reducing time spent on routine work so attorneys can spend time on strategy, business development, and client engagement. Finally, adoption requires thoughtful change management. Attorneys must build trust in the outputs while maintaining professional standards and reviewing outputs for accuracy. Firms are most successful when they begin with small wins such as drafting assistance with emails and letters before moving into areas that require heavier judgment.

The near future

For us, looking to the future means the "near future". We stress the near future because we doubt too many can predict exactly how the law industry will look in five to ten years, except to say it will be very different. Looking ahead, genAI is not simply another tool, it is a mindset shift. Drafting will become increasingly context-aware, drawing not just from legal precedent but from firm-specific patterns and client preferences. Predictive analytics will become embedded, offering insight into litigation outcomes, deal risks, and regulatory changes. We think the progression is clear – early automation showed the value of reducing redundancy and streamlining clerical work. GenAI builds on that foundation by enabling attorneys to work not just faster but smarter. Legal expertise is not replaced, but supplemented. The lawyers who adopt these tools reduce time spent on mundane administrative tasks and more time advising, strategizing, and providing more value-added services. We remember a meeting that one of us attended in 2023 where a Microsoft genAI ChatGPT expert was asked, "Will AI put lawyers out of work?" He replied, "No, but it will put lawyers out of work who do not use ChatGPT".

We believe that firms that embrace this mindset shift will not only lower costs and improve workflows but they will deliver more transparent, actionable, and client-centered value. In doing so, they will redefine the standard for legal services in an era where intelligence and efficiency are no longer separate goals but part of the same solution. GenAI will be a competitive advantage for those who can jump into the lead in mastering this mindset. Some of the early leaders will be those using legal AI products, using for example the likes of Harvey AI, CoCounsel, and OpenAI's ChatGPT Enterprise, as well as third-party start-ups for niche practice areas.

However, we predict that in a few years all reasonably sized law firms will have access to the same leading products, so that product competitive advantage could well disappear. Competitive advantage will come down to the ability to utilize tools more efficiently and effectively and for those who can build better experience data sets in those practice areas and industry segments that they aspire to lead in. As put by Paul Hlivko,[5] "The test of AI isn't whether we can build something new, it's whether we can embed it deeply enough into business systems to generate durable and measurable value". Like Hlivko, we believe that open-source collaboration and government-backed research will continue to push AI towards commoditization, hence the loss of the AI tools themselves being the competitive advantage.

In the future, will there will only be a few major developers who can afford the immense R&D expenditures to remain leaders? Will today's leaders in legal still be around? Will the likes of Microsoft, Google, and Salesforce dominate and will legal vendors be minor players with them all? Will Thomson Reuters and Lexis simply disappear in the legal world? Just as in the 1990s, when the legal industry's beloved Wordperfect was replaced with Word, will Microsoft also drive its genAI+ products into being the "AI products of choice" in the future legal industry, regardless of their present-day positioning? The pace of innovation is moving almost at the speed of light, so how do we develop the best strategy to stay in the race? Do we just hitch our wagon to Microsoft and hang on? As Hlivko hypothesizes, start-ups may push innovation forward but incumbents control enterprise budgets, IT integration, and distribution.

As a final word of caution – or relief, depending on one's current viewpoint

– the *Wall Street Journal*[6] reported that "95% of organizations surveyed are getting no return on their AI product investments. A University of Chicago economics paper found AI chatbots had no significant impact on workers' earnings, recorded hours, or wages at 7,000 Danish workplaces".

So, will it all be a big flop? Will we just absorb the costs of investment into legal genAI+ and make those costs part of our "cost of doing business" and try and recapture that cost via the rates we apply to our billable hours, just as we tried to capture Lexis and Westlaw research costs decades ago? In 2018, Procopio was recovering 71 percent of its legal research expense. In 2024, that percentage had dropped to 21 percent. A $3 hourly rate increase per lawyer would have handled the difference – so maybe we will all just do the same again with genAI. Adding $5 or $10 per hour per year to every lawyer's rate would handle our cost of annual tech expenditures... no big deal. But how will we handle the potential 15-50 percent reduction in the billable hour revenue that could be coming in the near future with advanced genAI tools?

To end with another quote from Ralph Baxter, "I think what's going to happen here is the market's going to end up paying less than it's now paying, but the smartest law firms are going to organize themselves so they can still make as much money if not more".[7] It therefore makes sense to plan your law firm to make sure they are one of the survivors.

References

1   Death of the Billable Hour: Legal's $900B AI Repricing. Ethan Batraski, 2025. ethan.substack.com/p/death-of-the-billable-hour-legal-ai

2   "Profitability, The Concept of Managing on the Edge, and their Importance to a Regional Law Firm." James G. Perkins, *The Mechanics of Law Firm Profitability*, Ark Group, 2016. www.globelawandbusiness.com/books/the-mechanics-of-law-firm-profitability-people-process-and-technology

3   Navigating Pricing in an Uncertain Legal Economy: Mark Medice, Principal, Law Vision: Lessons From the 2025 Strategic Pricing Law Firm Survey, 2025. https://lawvision.com/navigating-pricing-in-an-uncertain-legal-economy-lessons-from-the-2025-strategic-pricing-law-firm-survey/

4   Former Orrick Chair Says AI Poised to Entirely Transform Law: Ralph Baxter, Law360 Pulse, 2025. www.law360.com/pulse/articles/2347323/former-orrick-chair-says-ai-poised-to-entirely-transform-law

5   The AI Revolution Will Not Happen Overnight: Paul Hlviko, *HBR*, 24 June 2025. https://hbr.org/2025/06/the-ai-revolution-wont-happen-overnight

6   AI Spending is at EPIC Levels. Will It Ever Pay Off. *Wall Street Journal*, 25 September 2025. www.wsj.com/tech/ai/ai-bubble-building-spree-55ee6128

7   See Note 4.

Chapter 3:
Aligning client expectations with value perception

By Stéphanie Hamon, global head of legal external engagement, HSBC

Introduction

In today's legal services landscape, aligning client expectations with perceived value is essential to building trust, ensuring satisfaction, and maintaining long-term relationships. Legal service providers must move beyond traditional billing models and embrace approaches that prioritize outcomes, transparency, and collaboration. This chapter outlines a methodology for aligning client expectations with value perception, detailing key steps and providing practical recommendations.

Value is outcome-driven and context-specific

In the evolving legal services landscape, clients no longer equate value with the number of hours billed or the seniority of the lawyer assigned. Instead, they increasingly define value by the outcomes achieved and the strategic impact delivered. This shift reflects a broader trend across professional services, where clients expect tailored, business-aligned solutions rather than commoditized legal advice.

Understanding what clients truly value

Value is inherently subjective and varies not only from client to client but also from matter to matter. For some, value may mean cost predictability and budget adherence. For others, it may be about speed to market, regulatory risk mitigation, or the ability to unlock commercial opportunities. In high-stakes litigation, value might be defined by a favorable judgment or settlement; in transactional work, it could be the seamless execution of a cross-border deal under tight timelines.

This variability underscores the importance of engaging clients early to understand their specific goals, risk appetite, and success criteria. Legal providers must ask the right questions. What does success look like for this matter? What are the business drivers behind this instruction? What constraints – financial, operational, or reputational – must be considered?

From generic delivery to bespoke solutions

Generic service delivery models are no longer sufficient. Clients expect legal advice that is not only technically sound but also commercially relevant and operationally feasible. This requires providers to move beyond legal analysis and into the realm of strategic partnership. It also demands a deep understanding of the client's industry, internal pressures, and broader business objectives.

The role of legal operations and design thinking

Legal operations teams (or skillset) can play a critical role in translating client expectations into actionable service delivery models. By applying design thinking principles, legal providers can co-create solutions with clients that are intuitive, efficient, and aligned with business needs. This might involve mapping the client journey, identifying pain points, and redesigning workflows to eliminate friction.

Moreover, legal operations methodology often acts as an internal consultant toolkit, helping clients articulate what value means to them and how it should be measured. This includes developing key performance indicators (KPIs), service level agreements (SLAs), and feedback mechanisms that ensure continuous alignment.

Scoping as a strategic lever

Robust matter scoping is the foundation of value-based engagement. It enables legal providers to define the scope of work clearly, allocate resources appropriately, and price services in a way that reflects the value delivered. Effective scoping also fosters mutual accountability and reduces the risk of misalignment or scope creep.

Scoping should not be a one-time exercise. It must be revisited throughout the matter lifecycle to accommodate changes in client priorities, emerging risks, or new information. This iterative approach ensures that the legal team remains responsive, and the client continues to perceive value in the engagement.

Ultimately, aligning with client-defined value requires a mindset shift – from delivering legal outputs to enabling business outcomes. It calls for empathy, curiosity, and a willingness to challenge traditional models. Legal providers that embrace this approach will not only meet but exceed client expectations, earning their trust and loyalty in the process.

Pricing models must reflect value, not time

The legal industry is undergoing a fundamental shift in how services are priced. For decades, the billable hour has been the dominant model, offering a seemingly straightforward way to measure legal work. However, this model is increasingly viewed as outdated and misaligned with what clients value. It rewards time spent rather than outcomes achieved, and it often fails to provide the transparency, predictability, and alignment that modern legal departments demand.

Clients today are looking for pricing models that reflect the value of the service delivered – not the effort expended. This has led to a growing adoption of alternative fee arrangements (AFAs) and, more recently, effective fee arrangements (EFAs). While AFAs encompass any pricing model that deviates from the hourly rate – such as fixed fees, capped fees, or success-based pricing – EFAs go a step further. They are designed to align pricing with the value of the output, not just the structure of the input.

From AFAs to EFAs – a higher standard

EFAs set a higher bar than traditional AFAs. While many AFAs are still calculated based on estimated hours (essentially repackaging the billable hour), EFAs require a more thoughtful approach. They are built around the value that the legal service delivers to the client – whether that's a renegotiated contract, a successful litigation outcome, or a regulatory compliance strategy that avoids future risks.

The key to a successful EFA is understanding what the client values most in a given matter. This could be speed (e.g., in a cybersecurity breach response), industry expertise (e.g., in a complex regulatory environment), or even the mode of delivery (e.g., through a shared knowledge platform rather than traditional memos). Identifying these value drivers at the outset allows legal providers to structure pricing that reflects the true worth of their contribution.

The role of scoping and smart resourcing

EFAs depend on clear, granular scoping. Breaking a matter down into its component deliverables and associated workstreams enables both parties to see where the cost lies and what will be delivered in return. This not only facilitates more accurate pricing but also sets clear expectations, reducing the risk of scope creep and billing disputes.

Smart resourcing is another critical element. EFAs should be built on the assumption that legal work will be delivered in the most efficient way possible. This might involve using a mix of senior and junior lawyers, leveraging alternative legal service providers (ALSPs), or incorporating legal technology to automate routine tasks. The goal is to ensure that the right work is done by the right people at the right cost.

Incentivizing outcomes, not inputs

One of the most powerful aspects of EFAs is their ability to incentivize the right behaviors. Under a billable hour model, there is little incentive to work efficiently or to innovate. In contrast, EFAs reward legal providers for delivering results. This creates a more collaborative, trust-based relationship between client and provider – one that is focused on shared goals rather than time tracking.

For example, a gainshare model might reward a law firm with a bonus if they help a client close a deal ahead of schedule or under budget. A milestone-based fee might tie payments to the achievement of specific deliverables, such as the completion of due diligence or the filing of a regulatory submission. These models align the interests of both parties and create a more strategic partnership.

Building trust through transparency

EFAs also promote transparency. By agreeing on pricing and deliverables upfront, clients gain greater visibility into what they are paying for and why. This reduces the likelihood of surprise invoices and fosters a sense of fairness and accountability. It also enables legal departments to better forecast their budgets and demonstrate value to internal stakeholders.

In a world where legal departments are under increasing pressure to do more with less, EFAs offer a compelling alternative to the billable hour. They provide a framework for delivering high-quality legal services in a way that is aligned with client priorities, financially sustainable for providers, and conducive to long-term relationships.

Scoping as the foundation of value-based engagement

In the context of modern legal service delivery, robust matter scoping is not just a procedural step – it is a strategic imperative. As clients increasingly demand pricing models that reflect value rather than time, scoping becomes the linchpin that connects expectations, deliverables, and commercial outcomes. It is the foundation upon which value-based engagements are built. Scoping has already appeared twice in this methodology thus far but here follows some detail.

Why scoping matters

Scoping is the process of defining the parameters of a legal matter before substantive work begins. It involves identifying the objectives, deliverables, timelines, assumptions, constraints, and potential risks associated with the engagement. When done well, scoping provides clarity for both the client and the legal provider, enabling accurate budgeting, appropriate resourcing, and realistic timelines.

Without proper scoping, legal matters are prone to scope creep, misaligned expectations, and billing disputes. These issues not only erode trust but also undermine the perceived value of the legal service. In contrast, a well-scoped matter sets the stage for a collaborative, transparent, and outcome-focused relationship.

Scoping and pricing – two sides of the same coin

Scoping is inextricably linked to pricing. AFAs and EFAs rely on a clear understanding of what work will be done, by whom, and within what timeframe. Whether the pricing model is a fixed fee, milestone-based, or gainshare, it cannot function effectively without a detailed scope.

For example, a fixed-fee arrangement for a regulatory investigation must account for the number of jurisdictions involved, the volume of documents to be reviewed, and the anticipated level of regulatory engagement. Without this information, the fee is little more than a guess – and the risk of misalignment is high.

Legal project management – bringing structure to scoping

Legal project management (LPM) offers a structured and disciplined approach to scoping and matter management. LPM borrows from traditional project management disciplines to bring rigor and predictability to legal work.

LPM involves planning and managing all aspects of a matter from start to finish, including deliverables, resources, budget, risks, and timelines. It is particularly valuable in complex or high-volume matters, where coordination and consistency are critical. It can equally prove beneficial when managing a large portfolio of smaller similar matters. By applying LPM principles, legal teams can create workflows, manage risks, and ensure that both in-house and external lawyers as well as other parties such as alternative legal suppliers or consultants are aligned on expectations.

LPM is increasingly being adopted by in-house legal teams as a way to improve efficiency, reduce costs, and enhance collaboration with external counsel. It enables legal departments to act as strategic business partners, delivering legal services in a manner that is efficient, predictable, and aligned with business goals.

Collaborative scoping – a two-way dialogue

Effective scoping is not a one-sided exercise. It requires input from both the client and the legal provider. Clients must articulate their objectives, constraints, and success criteria, while providers must draw on their experience to anticipate challenges, propose solutions, and suggest efficiencies.

This collaborative approach fosters mutual accountability. It ensures that both parties are aligned on what will be delivered, how it will be delivered, and what success looks like. It also creates a shared understanding of the risks and trade-offs involved, enabling more informed decision-making.

Scoping as a living document

Scoping should not be static. As a matter progresses, new information may emerge, priorities may shift, and external factors may change. A flexible, iterative approach to scoping allows the legal team to adapt to these changes while maintaining alignment with the client.

Regular check-ins, status updates, and scope reviews are essential to ensure that the engagement remains on track. These touchpoints provide an opportunity to recalibrate expectations, adjust timelines, and manage emerging risks – thereby preserving the integrity of the value-based engagement.

Communication and expectation management

In the delivery of legal services, communication is not just a soft skill – it is a strategic tool. Clear, early, and continuous communication is the cornerstone of successful legal engagements. It underpins trust, ensures alignment, and enables agility in the face of evolving client needs. As legal departments become more sophisticated and outcome-focused, the expectation for proactive, transparent, and structured communication has never been higher.

Setting the tone early

The foundation of effective communication is laid before the matter even begins. During the onboarding or instruction phase, legal providers must engage in a detailed dialogue with the client to understand their objectives, constraints, and success criteria. This includes clarifying the scope of work, timelines, budget expectations, and preferred communication channels. It is also the time to agree on how progress will be reported, how risks will be escalated, and how changes to scope or budget will be handled.

This initial alignment is critical. It sets the tone for the engagement and helps prevent misunderstandings later. It also demonstrates a commitment to partnership and accountability – qualities that clients increasingly value in their legal providers.

Maintaining momentum through regular updates

Once the matter is underway, communication must be continuous and structured. This includes regular check-ins, status updates, and milestone reviews. These touchpoints serve multiple purposes – they keep the client informed, provide an opportunity to recalibrate expectations, and allow for early identification of issues.

Legal project management (LPM) tools and dashboards can be particularly useful in this context. They provide real-time visibility into matter status, budget consumption, and upcoming deliverables. This transparency not only builds trust but also empowers clients to make informed decisions.

In high-volume or complex matters, a communication plan should be developed and agreed upon at the outset. This plan should specify the frequency, format, and content of updates, as well as the roles and responsibilities of each party. For example, weekly email summaries might be appropriate for a fast-moving transaction, while monthly steering committee meetings might be better suited for a long-term regulatory engagement.

Managing expectations proactively

Expectation management is not a one-time event – it is a continuous process. As matters evolve, new information may emerge, priorities may shift, and external factors may change. Legal providers must be proactive in communicating these developments and their implications. This includes flagging risks early, proposing mitigation strategies, and seeking client input on key decisions.

Clients, for their part, must also play an active role. They should articulate their evolving needs, provide timely feedback, and be transparent about internal dynamics that may affect the engagement. This two-way communication fosters mutual accountability and ensures that both parties remain aligned.

The role of feedback loops

Feedback is a critical component of expectation management. It provides a mechanism for continuous improvement and helps identify areas where communication or service delivery can be enhanced. Feedback should be solicited at key milestones and at the conclusion of the matter. It should also be acted upon – demonstrating that the provider values the client's input and is committed to evolving their approach.

Some legal departments have formalized this process through client satisfaction surveys, net promoter scores (NPS), or post-matter reviews. Others use more informal methods, such as debrief calls or feedback forms. Regardless of the format, the goal is the same – to learn, adapt, and improve.

Building a culture of transparency

Ultimately, effective communication and expectation management require a cultural shift. Legal providers must move away from reactive, ad hoc communication and toward a more deliberate, client-centric approach. This means being transparent about challenges, honest about limitations, and open to feedback.

It also means investing in the tools, processes, and training needed to support this shift. This might include communication skills workshops, LPM certifications, or the adoption of collaboration platforms like Microsoft Teams or Slack.

Performance metrics and accountability

As legal departments evolve into more strategic, data-driven functions, the demand for measurable performance from external legal providers has intensified. Clients are no longer satisfied with anecdotal assessments or vague assurances of quality. Instead, they expect clear, quantifiable evidence that their legal partners are delivering value, meeting expectations, and continuously improving.

The rise of data-driven legal management

Modern legal departments are increasingly adopting legal operations frameworks that emphasize metrics, dashboards, and performance tracking. This shift mirrors broader trends in corporate procurement and vendor management, where data is used to drive decisions, justify budgets, and manage risk. In this environment, legal providers must be prepared to demonstrate their value through objective, client-relevant metrics.

Key performance indicators (KPIs) are central to this approach. Common KPIs include:

- *Budget adherence.* Was the matter delivered within the agreed budget or fee cap?
- *Responsiveness.* How quickly did the provider respond to queries or deliverables?
- *Quality of advice.* Was the legal advice accurate, actionable, and more importantly aligned with business needs?
- *Innovation and value-adds.* Did the provider offer tools, templates, training, or process improvements?
- *Client satisfaction.* How did the client rate the overall experience?

These metrics should be agreed upon at the outset of the engagement and reviewed regularly. They should also be tailored to the specific matter type and client priorities. For example, in a high-volume contract review project, turnaround time and consistency might be more important than legal complexity. In contrast, for a strategic M&A deal, commercial insight and risk management may take precedence.

Building a performance framework

To ensure accountability, many legal departments are implementing structured performance management frameworks. These frameworks typically include:

- *Service Level Agreements (SLAs).* Formal commitments on response times, deliverables, and escalation procedures.
- *Scorecards.* Periodic evaluations of provider performance across multiple dimensions.
- *Post-matter reviews.* Debriefs that capture lessons learned and areas for improvement.
- *Net Promoter Scores (NPS).* Simple metrics that gauge client satisfaction and loyalty.

Some organizations also use tiered panel structures, where firms must meet certain performance thresholds to remain on the panel or qualify for premium work. This creates a healthy level of competitive tension and incentivizes continuous improvement.

Transparency and trust

Performance metrics are not just about accountability – they are also about building trust. When providers are transparent about their performance, they demonstrate a commitment to excellence and a willingness to be held to high standards. This transparency fosters stronger relationships and positions the provider as a true partner rather than a transactional vendor.

It also enables more constructive conversations. If a matter goes over budget or a deliverable is delayed, having a shared set of metrics allows both parties to analyze what happened, why, and how to prevent it in the future. This data-driven approach reduces finger-pointing and supports a culture of continuous improvement.

Leveraging technology

Technology plays a critical role in performance management. Legal spend management platforms offer real-time visibility into billing, matter progress, and provider performance. These tools can automate reporting, flag anomalies, and generate insights that would be difficult to obtain manually. One could almost venture they will enable in-house legal teams to build their own pricing catalogue for future work they will outsource.

Some legal departments are also integrating performance data into broader enterprise dashboards, allowing legal to demonstrate its contribution to business goals. For example, linking legal KPIs to procurement savings, compliance outcomes, or revenue enablement can help elevate the function's strategic profile.

A two-way street

Finally, it's important to recognize that performance management is a two-way street. Just as clients evaluate their providers, providers should also be encouraged to give feedback on the client's processes, communication, and collaboration. This mutual accountability creates a more balanced relationship and helps both sides improve.

Smart resourcing and panel management

As legal departments strive to become more agile and value-driven, they are rethinking how legal work is allocated across their provider ecosystem. The traditional reliance on a fixed panel of firms, refreshed every few years, is giving way to a more dynamic and strategic approach to resourcing. Clients are increasingly focused on ensuring that the right work is done by the right provider with the right capabilities – whether that's a global law firm, a regional boutique, or an ALSP.

The shift toward strategic resourcing

This evolution reflects a broader trend toward legal departments operating more like business units. Rather than defaulting to legacy relationships or prestige-based selection, clients are now segmenting legal work by complexity, risk, and value – and matching it to the most appropriate resource. This enables better cost control, improved outcomes, and greater alignment with business priorities.

For example, high-volume, low-risk tasks such as contract abstraction or e-discovery may be routed to ALSPs or in-house centers of excellence, while high-stakes litigation or regulatory matters remain with top-tier firms. This segmentation allows legal teams to optimize spend and ensure that each provider is playing to their strengths.

Evolving panel structures

Panel management is also becoming more fluid. Instead of rigid, multi-year panel appointments, many organizations are adopting rolling or tiered models that allow for greater flexibility and responsiveness. These models emphasize continuous performance evaluation and the ability to onboard or offboard providers based on evolving needs and performance.

Key features of modern panel structures include:
- *Capability-based tiers.* Providers are grouped by expertise, geography, or matter type, rather than a one-size-fits-all panel or by supplier categories such as international law firms, regional law firms, boutique firms, ALSP, etc.
- *Performance-linked access.* Providers must meet defined performance thresholds to remain eligible for work.
- *Innovation incentives.* Firms that demonstrate process improvements, technology adoption, or value-adds may be rewarded with additional work or strategic partnerships.

Building a resourcing framework

To support this smarter approach to resourcing, legal departments are developing structured frameworks that guide provider selection and engagement. These frameworks typically include:

- *Matter triage protocols.* Decision trees or intake tools that help route work to the right provider based on complexity, urgency, and cost sensitivity.
- *Preferred provider matrices.* Visual maps of which firms or ALSPs are preferred for specific matter types or jurisdictions.
- *Engagement playbooks.* Standardized guidelines for scoping, pricing, and managing engagements across different provider types.

Technology as an enabler

Technology plays a critical role in enabling smart resourcing. Legal spend management platforms, workflow tools, and matter management systems provide the data and visibility needed to make informed decisions. These tools can track provider performance, flag inefficiencies, and support real-time allocation of work.

Some legal departments are also integrating AI-powered tools to assist with matter classification, risk scoring, and provider recommendations – further enhancing their ability to allocate work intelligently.

Relationship management and collaboration

Smart resourcing is not just about efficiency – it's also about building stronger, more collaborative relationships with providers. By aligning expectations, sharing performance data, and fostering open communication, legal departments can create a culture of continuous improvement and mutual accountability.

This approach positions providers as strategic partners rather than transactional vendors, enabling more innovative, business-aligned legal service delivery.

Governance and internal alignment

As legal departments mature into strategic business enablers, effective governance and internal alignment have become foundational to managing external legal spend and driving operational excellence. Without clear internal processes and stakeholder coordination, even the most sophisticated legal technology or panel strategy will fall short.

The need for internal cohesion

Governance in legal operations is about more than compliance – it's about clarity, consistency, and control. Legal departments must ensure that internal stakeholders, including legal, procurement, finance, and business units, are aligned on how legal services are instructed, delivered, and evaluated. This requires well-defined policies for provider selection, matter scoping, budgeting, and performance review.

In many organizations, the absence of such alignment leads to fragmented decision-making, inconsistent provider engagement, and missed opportunities for cost control and value creation. A robust governance framework ensures that legal work is triaged appropriately, routed to the right provider, and managed in line with strategic priorities.

Building a governance framework

A strong governance model typically includes:
- *Instruction protocols.* Clear guidelines on who can instruct external counsel, under what circumstances, and through which channels.
- *Approval workflows.* Defined thresholds for spend approvals, escalation paths, and delegated authority.
- *Matter management standards.* Consistent approaches to scoping, budgeting, and tracking legal work.
- *Provider engagement policies.* Criteria for selecting, onboarding, and evaluating external providers.

These elements should be codified in a legal operations playbook or policy manual, ensuring consistency across teams and jurisdictions.

Cross-functional collaboration

Governance is not the sole responsibility of the legal team. Effective alignment requires close collaboration with procurement, finance, compliance, and business stakeholders. For example:
- Procurement brings rigor to vendor selection and contract negotiation.
- Finance ensures alignment with budgeting, forecasting, and cost control processes.
- Business units provide context on commercial priorities and risk appetite.

Establishing cross-functional working groups or steering committees can help maintain alignment, resolve conflicts, and drive continuous improvement.

Technology as an enabler – not a substitute
While legal technology can support governance – through matter management systems, spend analytics, and workflow automation – it cannot replace the need for clear processes and stakeholder buy-in. Technology should be implemented only after internal processes are well understood and optimized.

Tools such as intake portals, contract lifecycle management (CLM) systems, and legal spend platforms can reinforce governance by embedding controls into day-to-day workflows. However, their success depends on user adoption, data quality, and integration with broader enterprise systems.

Change management and cultural alignment
Governance initiatives often require a shift in mindset – from reactive to proactive, from siloed to collaborative. Successful transformation depends on "winning hearts and minds". This means engaging stakeholders early, communicating the rationale for change, and providing training and support.

Change management should be embedded into governance programs, with clear messaging, leadership sponsorship, and feedback loops to monitor adoption and address resistance.

Measuring success
To ensure accountability and continuous improvement, legal departments should track governance KPIs such as:
- Percentage of matters initiated through approved channels.
- Compliance with budgeting and approval protocols.
- Time to instruct and onboard providers.
- Stakeholder satisfaction with legal service delivery.

These metrics can be used to refine processes, identify training needs, and demonstrate the value of managing your external spend and your broader ecosystem to the broader business.

Collaboration and relationship building
In today's complex legal ecosystem, clients increasingly expect their legal service providers to act as strategic partners rather than transactional

vendors. This shift demands a deeper level of collaboration – one that is rooted in trust, transparency, and shared purpose. High-performing providers distinguish themselves not only through technical excellence but also through their ability to co-create solutions, share insights, and adapt to evolving client needs.

From vendor to partner
The most successful legal relationships are those that transcend the traditional client–provider dynamic. Clients value providers who invest in understanding their business, anticipate challenges, and proactively offer solutions. This requires a mindset shift – from delivering legal advice in isolation to embedding legal expertise within the broader business context.

Empathy, agility, and ecosystem collaboration are now essential leadership traits for smooth legal operations. Providers must demonstrate a willingness to listen, adapt, and innovate alongside their clients. This includes embracing hybrid delivery models, integrating diverse talent, and aligning incentives to drive mutual success.

Institutionalizing collaboration
To embed collaboration into the fabric of legal service delivery, many organizations are implementing structured relationship frameworks. These may include:
- *Joint planning sessions.* Regular meetings to align on strategic goals, upcoming matters, and resource planning.
- *Feedback loops.* Mechanisms such as post-matter reviews, NPS, and client satisfaction surveys to capture insights and drive continuous improvement.
- *Innovation forums.* Dedicated spaces to explore new technologies, process improvements, and co-developed solutions.
- *Shared success metrics.* Agreed KPIs that reflect both legal outcomes and business impact.

These frameworks help legal teams move from reactive service delivery to proactive partnership, enabling them to better support business objectives and manage risk.

The role of legal operations
Legal operations plays a critical role in fostering collaboration. By acting as

a bridge between legal, procurement, finance, and the business, legal ops professionals help align expectations, streamline communication, and ensure accountability. There are a number of legal operations initiatives in the industry that provide a platform for sharing best practices, exploring emerging trends, and building community across the legal ecosystem.

Moreover, as noted in the CLOC 2025 State of the Industry report,[1] the rise of Legal Ops 3.0 places greater emphasis on soft skills such as emotional intelligence, storytelling, and enterprise collaboration. These capabilities are essential for building trust and navigating the complexities of modern legal service delivery.

Technology as a collaboration enabler

Technology can enhance collaboration by providing shared platforms for communication, document management, and performance tracking. Tools like contract lifecycle management (CLM) systems, legal spend platforms, and client portals enable real-time visibility and foster transparency. However, technology must always be underpinned by clear processes and strong relationships to be truly effective.

A cultural shift

Ultimately, collaboration and relationship building require a cultural shift on both sides. Legal providers must move from billing hours to delivering impact. Clients must engage in open, ongoing dialogue and be willing to invest in long-term partnerships. When both parties embrace this model, pricing becomes a strategic enabler of trust, efficiency, and shared success.

Conclusion

Aligning client expectations with value perception is a multifaceted process that requires a deep understanding of client needs, transparent communication, and a commitment to delivering outcomes. By adopting value-driven pricing models, engaging in robust scoping, maintaining continuous communication, and leveraging performance metrics, legal providers can build trust and foster long-term relationships with their clients. The key to success lies in collaboration, flexibility, and a shared commitment to achieving strategic goals.

References

1   CLOC 2025 State of the Industry report: https://cloc.org/2025-soti-report/

Chapter 4:

Applying value-related qualities for better fee arrangements and greater client satisfaction

By Steven A. Lauer

When corporate clients deal with their counsel, especially their external counsel, the cost of the service that they need typically matters to some degree. After all, the legal service matters to a company for one purpose – to help that organization realize a business goal, whether in litigation, a transaction, or designing a new product or service. When discussing possible retention with a prospective client or an ongoing relationship, the lawyers must keep in mind the client's imperative that the legal service help achieve a particular result that is nonlegal and that the cost of doing so must be commensurate with that objective.

Unfortunately, too often lawyers seem to lose sight of that point. They often get caught up in the weeds of the legal work and fail to connect it to the client's business perspective and objective. As a former in-house attorney, I've seen too many lengthy, overly complex, and convoluted memoranda from law firms that went far beyond answering the business question while exploring the minutiae of the legal issues that the lawyers considered relevant to that task, even if only tangentially.

That disconnect between lawyers' thinking and their clients' thinking has led to much discontent among companies. This, in turn, has led to consternation among lawyers as they face that discontent and some dissatisfaction on the part of consumers of corporate legal service.

In order to align the thinking of clients and lawyers, lawyers should adopt the clients' view of the lawyers' efforts. Since the client is the recipient of the lawyers' service, the client's needs for which that service is ordered should largely affect the form and utility of the service, including its cost.

The absence of a measure of "value" for what lawyers do for their corporate clients

The fee charged by counsel to a corporate client occupies a central position in the relationship between them, whether that relationship has existed for a long time or it arises for the current engagement. The fee relates to all aspects of the manner in which the client and its counsel work together. Accordingly, that fee must be examined in that context and understood in light of the client's goals for the engagement – very importantly, in the context of the client's business goals and its expectations for the project(s) in question. The fee structure also impacts how counsel contributes to the achievement of the client's business goal for the matter.

While most discussion regarding legal fees revolves around the amount of the fee itself, the more important point to bear in mind relates to the value of the service provided.[1] While all clients would prefer to pay less for legal service, many if not most would pay a fee if that fee represented sufficient "value" for the client, almost regardless of the actual number in question.

The relevant point for many clients is that the fees charged by outside lawyers for work performed on behalf of the clients often bear no direct relationship to the clients' views as to how that work benefits the organization. From the invoices that they receive from their counsel, they often cannot determine how well the work represented correlates to the business-related benefit that the client hopes to enjoy on account of those efforts.

The core issue generally relates to how fees are calculated. For most corporate clients, outside counsel's invoices represent a time-and-money calculation, whereby the number of hours devoted by counsel to the client's work is multiplied by a billing rate (usually on an hourly basis). Nowhere in that calculation does one find a place to incorporate the effect that the lawyers' work has on the purpose of the client's retention of the lawyers.

The result is that the client can only calculate the bottom-line effect of its lawyers' work on its behalf after the work has been completed and an invoice for that work received. While the work is being performed, the client is virtually unable to assess how closely that effort correlates to its expectations and its needs. It has no measurable means of assessing how much the lawyers' work equated with value and whether that was high or low. In many instances, clients who found themselves in that situation had few options. They could resort to negotiation after the fact, seeking a reduction in fees already billed or some compensatory trade, like a discount on a future invoice. The second alternative would be to seek new counsel for the matter in question (in which case the client might lose whatever benefit it might have had on account of the first firm's efforts) or for future matters. Either result has considerable negative consequences for the relationship between the client and its counsel, a relationship that has fiduciary overtones yet ends up in an adversarial situation as their interests do not coincide in respect of what the client owes the lawyers for their work on its behalf. The discontent that corporate clients feel with respect to the billings that they see from their outside counsel has a corrosive effect on that relationship.

For outside counsel, the lack of a measurement for the benefit that their work bestows on the client leaves them adrift. If they recognize the clients' unease, they may feel unable to address the basis for that unease – the clients' feeling that "fees are too high" or that they are untethered to the work itself. Consequently, the client will be asked to pay more than it thinks the work justifies or otherwise has no discernable connection to achieving its business goals for the matter in question.

The absence of a common understanding of value and the profession's reliance on time-based billing also disserves clients and disadvantages firms in another way. Clients trying to identify counsel for their matters have no gauge with which to measure how well different law firms might serve their needs, except by a time-consuming and inexact process of reviewing marketing material, online commentary, and asking other companies for their opinions. Firms' marketing material, of course, is less helpful because it all sounds similar in that every firm claims to be the best, but with few offering supportive data for that claim. Accordingly, companies seeking outside counsel are left to compare firms with the only metric available – the firm's billing rates.

This disconnect between price and value has been recognized for many years. In fact, in-house attorneys (for obvious reasons, it seems to me) have attempted to cut that Gordian knot in several ways. For example, several decades ago, law firms routinely sent their corporate clients invoices that contained only a single-line description for the work being billed, as "for professional services rendered", even if the bill totaled millions of dollars. In an effort to understand better what their companies were paying for, in-house attorneys began requesting greater itemization of that impenetrable phrase. This led, ultimately, to itemized bills that displayed the time spent on those matters, with that time broken into discrete time entries (often in the form of tenths of an hour). Over time, those invoices evolved into endless (it seemed) lists of time entries. The volume of entries and the granularity of the itemization became impenetrable with the overall service, leaving the reviewers of those bills as uncertain as they had been previously regarding the "value" that their companies received in exchange for the fees.

In 2008, the Association of Corporate Counsel (ACC) launched the ACC

Value Challenge to initiate a dialogue within the legal profession about value. The ACC didn't offer a definition of the term, hoping instead that an exchange of ideas and perspectives by lawyers in varying contexts (external practice and internal law departments, as examples) would lead to greater understanding across the legal profession of that concept. One might legitimately question whether that initiative achieved the goal that ACC had set.[2] Not much has changed in the intervening years to eliminate that confusion.

Many in the legal profession seem to support the idea of alternative fee arrangements in order to reduce the reliance on time-based billing and the opposing interests of clients and counsel that follow. Doing so has proven far more challenging than many expected or hoped, as evidenced by the continuing dominance of billing to corporate clients by the hourly rate (or fees based on another time-based factor).

It's time, then, to consider how lawyers and clients can examine and to measure how well the former's efforts benefit their corporate clients. When we speak of "value" of the service (in the gross sense of a single value for the entire service) in this context, of course, we have no system of measurement to use. This is particularly so in light of the very different perspectives of counsel and client mentioned above. For an outside attorney, the expenditure of time represents a legitimate "value" of the work and individual attorneys command disparate rates of compensation. The client, on the other hand, retains counsel in order to achieve a business goal and it assesses the lawyers' fees from that perspective.

Recognizing and taking advantage of the utility of value-related qualities

To start, we must recognize that, historically speaking, pricing decisions have been largely in the hands of outside counsel. Law firms set their hourly (or other) rates, rarely conferring with their clients about those rates or the mechanism by which those rates are determined or how they factor into the firm's invoices. Since "value" represents (or should represent) a client-centric view or perspective, we should look at those considerations from the vantage point of the client.

For the client and its internal counsel, the value of external counsel's efforts can be determined only by examining how well that work enabled or assisted the client to achieve its business objective of the effort. To the extent that the service did help the client achieve its stated objective, how does the fee compare to the degree to which the work contributed to that achievement? If, for example, counsel spend considerable time on and devote considerable attention to minor details of a transaction that the client views as a simple, straightforward, and familiar one, that client might view the lawyer as having expended more than a reasonable effort. It may well view the fees in an invoice as excessive. The client will feel that the value of that service will be less than it had wanted due to the excessive cost of achieving its objective. The benefit to the client must be the touchstone in any discussion of value.

Rather than try to assess a value for the legal service as a whole, we would benefit from recognizing that legal service benefits the client in a number of ways, which reflect the attributes of quality of the service. Each of those can be viewed on its own and, in many cases, measured in that way. One can identify multiple attributes of legal service that one can examine in this way. Here are some of the more significant ones:

- Expertise.
- Cost control.
- Understanding the client and its industry.
- Low cost.
- Consistency.
- Predictability.
- Speed of resolution or completion.
- Reliability.
- Responsiveness.
- Convenience.
- Security of data and other information.
- Certainty of an acceptable resolution.

Clearly, some of these and other attributes of legal service will matter more in some contexts or assignments than in others. The relative importance of those attributes will differ in different situations. Hypothesize a situation in which a company needs to preserve its intellectual property interest following the departure of a key employee who accepted a position with a competitor after downloading proprietary information. Due to the significance of that property and the rapidity with which it might be utilized by a competitor, not to mention the tests that courts would apply when asked to intervene, speed would be a primary consideration for the client when selecting counsel and embarking on the effort to protect its property. The company would likely consider much less important the fear of paying high hourly rates for its counsel. If the urgency were not so pronounced, budgetary concerns might rank higher.

Given that legal service includes many attributes that can, and often do, impact how well that work has a positive bottom-line impact on the client's business objective, how can lawyers use this perspective for the benefit of clients and themselves? How might the legal profession avail itself of these value-related qualities (VRQs) in serving its corporate clients?

Recognize also that each client may respond positively to multiple VRQs, with none of them excluding the others. Recognize as well that the relative importance of the VRQs will vary, both within the context of a specific assignment and, even more, from assignment to assignment. Finally, understand that different clients have varying expectations of their counsel in respect of the VRQs that they (the clients) deem most important.

All this means that counsel should approach each client and each retention as an opportunity to explore what truly matters to that client in that specific situation. If the discussion is frank and open, it should educate the attorney regarding that client's perspective on the expected legal service and, perhaps more important, how that service can best help the client to achieve its business objective for the assignment.

How do VRQs relate to the pricing of legal services? The obvious response is that the price of legal services should correlate to the client's value-related expectation. Unfortunately, when the price (the fee) charged is based on the amount of time that the lawyers spent on the matter, the client is left to determine whether such a correlation exists and, if so, how well the fee reflects the value of the work in the client's mind. Incorporating VRQs in the process of measuring value leads to a measurable, more reliable, and comparable means of making that determination.

If the work were described in ways that incorporate the client's views on its value, the client would be better able to assess the benefit that it realized from those efforts. VRQs can be used to categorize the ways in which the lawyers' work corresponded to the client's needs using value-related concepts.

VRQs can also enable more robust communications between corporate clients and their counsel about the work needed by the client. They can discuss the assignment in the context of the client's business and how that work should contribute to achieving the client's objectives, once again utilizing the client's own value-oriented profile and thinking.

VRQs possess another advantage over the nebulous concept of "value" of legal service – they are more granular. They also relate to specific traits of the service and the situation that are more measurable. That measurability may be the quality most useful in pricing. If, for example, a client wishes to design a fee arrangement that includes a baseline fee, such as a monthly retainer, and a bonus for achieving specific results that are consistent with its value concept, the premium portion might be designed to be due on reaching negotiated benchmarks reflective of the agreed-upon VRQs. The client and counsel can monitor whether the firm achieved those VRQs in providing the legal service. If it did, payment of the premium would be triggered.

Value-related qualities impact more than just fees, but all those effects relate to cost and value

Other ways in which VRQs can serve the interests of clients and counsel include the following, all of which relate to or affect pricing and fees and, ultimately, value.

First and foremost, VRQs enable the client and counsel to discuss and agree on important aspects of the purpose for which the client has retained (or is contemplating retaining) the firm. The client can express and the lawyers can understand the former's goals for the engagement and how the client expects or wants counsel to proceed. Those considerations should (and certainly will) affect the representation in multiple ways, including the fee itself. Consider, as one example, the client's ultimate goal. In the context of a dispute, a client generally wants to win. What that word means, though, can vary.

In litigation, while victory is often the expressed goal, that might mean different things to different people. This is particularly true of lawyers and their clients. If the client feels that an important business principle is at stake, then quick and complete vindication in a court of law may be the only acceptable outcome. Cost may not matter in that circumstance. In other situations, however, other outcomes might be preferable to the client.

Perhaps the client has become embroiled in a dispute or litigation with another party to a project in which the client is involved, in the midst of work on the project. The client wishes to buy time in the dispute in order to complete its work on the project and perhaps even before expending significant resources on the battle. A quick, decisive victory in the litigation could prove problematic if it complicates the relationship of the parties to that project. Engaging a firm known for unrestrained tactics in litigation and then expressing the desire to "win" may disserve the client's interests if that law firm's tactics cause the other party to prefer to sever the relationship with the client completely to trying to salvage it.

That simple word "win" does not suffice as instruction to counsel in litigation other than in the most straightforward situations. Business professionals do not speak in lawyer talk, and they might have in mind something far different from what a lawyer infers from an expressed desire to win in a situation. The client might wish to secure more time within which to negotiate a business resolution to a dispute, rather than an outright judicial victory. Even among experienced trial attorneys one might find varying interpretations of that simple word. The client's "real" goal should and will (if properly understood and taken into consideration) affect the relationship and the fee arrangement.

For many companies, putting aside "bet-the-company" situations, budgetary and cost concerns are ever-present and constitute a VRQ. Those issues relate directly to the fee arrangement between a company and its external counsel, yet their implications for that arrangement often receive inadequate attention. Understanding a client's need for cost control (a VRQ) would be important for counsel who hope to have a long-term relationship with that client.

As you can see, the importance of cost control as a VRQ varies, not only between different clients and companies, but even for one company in different contexts. This is an important point to keep in mind.

The parties also possess VRQs

While legal service has characteristics that we call VRQs, it's also important to understand that VRQs relate to the parties to the client/counsel relationship. All of these are relevant to a discussion of legal fees. The VRQs that affect the client's level of satisfaction with the lawyers' handling of its work are its "value drivers" for that engagement and they will be specific to the combination of the work, the client, and the counsel.

Here's an obvious example. Firms that specialize in litigation, whether handling large or small matters, develop some specific expertise. They develop a reputation for that expertise and it often serves as an excellent marketing tool, attracting potential clients with a need for such representation. Drilling down further, though, one realizes that not all litigation is the same and not all litigation firms are equal. Some become "go to" firms for major matters, especially bet-the-company assignments. That type of practice breeds a certain type of litigator, where cost is not important and a no-stone-unturned approach predominates in their thinking. That approach, however well it might work in those cases, will not serve a client as well when cost is an important consideration, like in a small slip-and-fall case or a simple landlord–tenant dispute. The selection of a firm that is known for the former type of case to handle the latter would be a mismatch based on the VRQs of the assignment and the firm. Not only would the budgetary impact be undesirable for the client, but the differing approaches to a dispute by the law firms can have dire negative implications. A firm that is accustomed to using "scorched-earth" tactics because it routinely handles its clients' bet-the-farm cases might approach a much less portentous dispute in the same way and alienate the other party.

The point to remember is that different firms, like different lawyers, have different skill sets. The client and the firm ought to consider how well the firm's capabilities match up against the needs of the project and the client's expectations. A mismatch might well lead to disappointment on the part of one or both of them. Using VRQs to examine that matchup would increase the probability of a good match for both.

The skill sets for which a firm becomes known might be designated its "strategic strengths". Those strengths represent some of its VRQs. Using those VRQs when selecting and retaining that firm leads to a greater alignment between the client's internal vision of value and its expectations in that regard and the reality that it will encounter during the engagement. The firm's behavior in the relationship and the service that it provides, both of which will reflect its strengths, will be consonant with the client's vision of the role for the firm.

It's also important to take into account the VRQs of the client. Some companies have in-house legal departments while others do not. A company that has lawyers on staff has internal resources that probably complement those of the law firms it retains. A corporate law department should, at a minimum, focus on managing the legal service for the organization so as to extract the most from it. Even among companies that have in-house law departments, though, the capabilities of those departments and the resources that they are able to deploy on the companies' behalf vary. This, in turn, will impact the ways in which those companies work with external counsel and where they draw the line between the internal resources deployed and the external resources retained.

A couple of examples should illustrate this. Two large life insurance companies competed head-to-head in the market, with the "winner" changing almost year-to-year. Despite having the same product and operating on a national basis, they took divergent approaches in respect of their law departments. One company had a large law department of several hundred attorneys while the other company had a much smaller department. This dichotomy was particularly notable in respect of the organizations' real estate investments. While both had sizeable portfolios of real estate assets, one company relied on a small cadre of inside counsel to manage the work of the outside firms that did the frontline work. The other company had a significant number of in-house attorneys dedicated to its real estate operations. Much of the work for that second company was completed internally, with outside counsel augmenting the internal resources on a planned basis.

Those disparate approaches to the same challenge in similar businesses had considerable impact on the companies' use and management of outside counsel and, ultimately, on the cost and various aspects of that resource and the service. The critical point is that different companies' capabilities and needs vary and their expectations regarding how counsel should service them also vary. Determining the optimal service model requires understanding the various ways in which the client, the counsel, and the matter in question relate and impact each other. Ultimately, selecting appropriate counsel for the assignment takes thought and research.

The search for value and the question of fees

The cost-control imperative in business is real. To understand it fully, though, one must step back and look at how the cost of a service (or a product, though that relates to an entirely separate discussion beyond the scope of this book) compares to what the consumer of that service gains as a result. If the lawyers' efforts enable a company to realize a great deal, which eclipses the fee charged, the client will have enjoyed great value. A vignette illustrates this point well.

"There is a story, perhaps apocryphal, of the corporation general counsel in the Midwest [of the United States] who asked [Clark] Clifford [former advisor to Presidents Harry Truman and Lyndon Johnson and Secretary of Defense] what his company should do concerning certain tax legislation. After several weeks, Clifford responded, 'Nothing,' and enclosed a bill for $20,000. Unaccustomed to the Clifford style, the general counsel testily wrote that for $20,000 he certainly was entitled to a more complete expla-

nation of the recommendation. He got it. 'Because I said so,' Clifford said in letter two, and billed the corporation for another $5,000."[3]

With his background, expertise and connections, Clark Clifford's advice carried great weight and proved valuable to many clients. The fee he charged, even while not using time-based billing, often paled in comparison to the benefit that the client gained. Though the client in that vignette did not have experience with Mr Clifford and only knew him by reputation, even advice not to act represented considerable benefit if acting might have caused negative consequences, as Mr Clifford believed.

That example, of course, is not of a common occurrence, yet it illustrates that value and price do not necessarily move in unison. Whether a fee represents sufficient value for the client is not a result solely of the number of dollars or euros paid.

Measuring the value that a client enjoys from its lawyers' work can be done more readily by using VRQs than by attempting to measure it in a "gross" fashion. Each exercise may need to take into account distinct VRQs, though, as the above discussion highlights. By doing so, however, both client and its counsel will gain a far better understanding of the work, the client's needs and expectations, and counsel's capabilities and contribution to the client's business activities.

The bottom line (and in business, it's always about the "bottom line") is that the fee arrangement between counsel and a corporate client should take into account various considerations. Those considerations should include VRQs agreed to by the parties. Discussing and determining the client's value-focused goals and how counsel can help the client realize those goals and the value that the lawyers can contribute to achieving its hoped-for result should then animate the form of the fee arrangement, the milestones that they will use to determine whether and how well they achieve the goals, and other relevant aspects of their relationship and the assignment.

Understanding the client's views on the lawyers' work would enable counsel to craft a fee arrangement with the client that incorporates the client's value-related needs and expectations. Identifying the VRQs that the client has in mind (whether consciously or not) would constitute the first step in doing so. Ultimately, using the VRQ concept in that way should also lead to more satisfied clients, a considerable benefit itself.

References

1   Paul Simon expressed this point well: "Ain't it strange the way we're ignorant, how we seek out bad advice. How we jigger it and figure it, mistaking value for the price." © 2010 Paul Simon, "So Beautiful or So What".

2   One consultant noted two years after ACC's launch of the initiative that "much remains confused and unclear about that term [i.e., 'value']." Morrison, "Making some sense out of the value gap," *The National Law Journal*, 9 November 2009.

3   Goulden, J., *The Superlawyers: The Small and Powerful World of the Great Washington Law Firms*, New York, Weybright and Talley, 1972, p. 71.

Chapter 5:
The role of data and analytics in modern legal pricing

By Tanbir Jasimuddin, freelance finance and analytics transformation director

Client demand – the billable hour must die

Let's be honest – we've heard this one before. The billable hour still dominates. According to a recent Legal Value Network survey, firms still handle 75 percent or more of their work on a billable hour basis.[1]

From a client perspective, the problem with the billable hour is that, firstly, there is no certainty how much they will be charged. They find it hard to budget for it. Furthermore, the lawyer is not motivated to achieve an outcome in the best interests of the client. In the client's mind, they are getting paid regardless.

Most of us who have worked in the profession know that this is rarely the case from a lawyer's point of view. As a consequence, they will overcompensate. They will provide a gold-plated service, when the client only asked for bronze. They will write-off a large number of hours that they have worked to offer what they perceive to be a palatable price for the client.

Both the client and the lawyer are losing.

Over the years, many different pricing models have been tried as a way to address the above issues, collectively known as "alternate fee arrangements". Examples include:

- Flat / fixed fees.
- Capped fees.
- Contingent fees.
- Success fees.
- Retainers.
- Volume discounts / rebates.
- Risk sharing.

These aren't niche practices. A 2021 study showed that 84 percent of law firms offered some form of AFA.[2] Indeed, growth is projected. In 2024, firms were charging 34 percent more cases on a flat fee basis compared to 2016.[3]

Market expectations and demand are for the eventual move away from the billable hour in favor of cost predictability and value alignment. Law firms have resisted this change. Historically, as the majority of firms continued with the billable hour, clients had very little choice. However, as more firms are offering an increasing volume of AFA-based work, clients now have more options. Firms with AFAs will start to take business away from the ones that do not. With this gradual shift now happening, firms need to adapt or risk losing market share to competitors who embrace transparency and predictability.

Data and analytics – the cornerstone of modern legal pricing

According to McKinsey research, organizations using analytics for pricing will achieve significant financial gains,[4] including an increase in revenue of between two and seven percent and an increase in margin of between five and ten percent. Comprehensive AI-powered approaches can uplift revenues by between ten and 20 percent.

Among the (many) other reasons for the growth in AFA is the increasing use of analytics within law firms. AFAs are considerably more sophisticated to calculate than the billable hour. Anyone who has had to endure the monthly 250-page printed report of out-of-date and near-useless financial stats will attest that, historically, law firm finance departments have had neither the skills, nor the data platforms, to provide any insight into pricing.

Profitable implementation of AFAs needs a deeper level of financial and operational expertise to be able to track the cost of delivering the legal services and the value those services represent to the client. This requires scrutiny of not just the timesheets, but also resource allocation patterns, operational efficiency, and historical profitability of similar matters. In addition, we need to understand what the client perceives as value. To deliver this, finance / pricing teams need to adopt greater skill levels and technology platforms.

From a technology perspective, legal practice management systems (PMS) lag quite significantly behind other sectors. It is the author's opinion that the two largest players have still to offer a "true" multi-tenant cloud platform. There are significant shortcomings in their financial management functionalities.

However, there is momentum. Even before the GenAI "panic", there was a greater acknowledgement of the need to improve the finance function to move beyond a back-office function to become a value-adding partner, supported by a more able analytics stack. Under pressure from both their firms and the growing competence driven by accountancy bodies, finance teams have moved beyond basic bean counting and compliance tasks to more value-added tasks – including providing insights into areas such as strategy and pricing.

From a technology perspective, we have seen some significant shifts in the data analytics market over the last decade. This area has become more mature – both in terms of the technology available, and more importantly, the skills available to deploy them. Analytics technology vendors have become relatively platform-agnostic. This means that you can choose platforms that are not bundled with your PMS. Technology is no longer a barrier in pricing analytics.

Data-informed pricing

Law firms are in a fortunate position. A massive amount of information is generated and stored. Very few sectors invest as much effort in recording virtually every minute of what a fee earner does. Of course, there are challenges with the ability to mine information from the raw data and the ability to make it usable. However, there is a goldmine of information that can be used to inform pricing decisions and optimize resource allocation, including lawyer performance metrics, historical matter data, matter outcomes, and historic financial data.

Setting a price goes hand in hand with the cost of delivery – optimizing internal operations is as vital to profitability as the price. The profitability of a fixed fee case, for example, hinges on the firm's ability to deliver the required services at an internal cost below the agreed fee(s). This is especially important with AFAs where the firm carries more risk related to efficiencies.

Delivery issues include inefficiencies in resource allocation, e.g. assigning partners to tasks that could be done by associates, overstaffing matters, or allowing bottlenecks to develop. These inflate the cost of delivery and erode profitability.

Data analytics provides insights into these areas and allows you to address them. There are three broad areas where analytics is deployed:
- Baselining through rigorous analysis of historical case data.
- Incorporating people analytics for more profitable resource allocation.
- Tailoring pricing to client needs and value perception.

Let's look at each.

Baselining through rigorous analysis of historical case data

The first step in informing a pricing decision is understanding "How much did it cost us to deliver it in the past?". Evaluating the profitability of past fee structures will inform the design of future arrangements.

Historic data can be analyzed through multiple dimensions – matter type, rates applied, client / sector, hours logged, hours written off, and hours billed. The more dimensions you are able to analyze, the more accurately you will be able to benchmark your initial price.

The second step is to get more granular. The data will provide insights into a case lifecycle, duration of the phases, and costs associated with specific tasks.

Third, you can perform a postmortem on past matters to understand where you can become more efficient. These three areas combined will give you a baseline of how much it will cost to deliver a case. This knowledge is critical to setting a price that is profitable.

Note that there are always nuances to consider. Looking at past costs alone is insufficient. Judgement is required to understand the new case and the additional variables that it will bring. Data-driven pricing, where we are relying on the data to give us an answer, is science. However, data-informed pricing is a combination of both science and art.

Incorporating people analytics for more profitable resource allocation

To maximize profitability, you need to ensure effective resource allocation – i.e. the right people, at the right level, doing the right level of work. The aim is to avoid both the over-utilization of expensive resources and the under-utilization of available capacity elsewhere.

As lawyers rise through the ranks, their salaries tend to increase at a faster rate than their charge-out rates. As a result, their profitability, on an hourly basis, declines. For a large proportion of firms, the "sweet spot" of the highest percentage hourly profitability is between one- and four-years' post-qualification experience (although this does vary from firm to firm). Therefore, you need to ensure that these grades are performing as much of the work as possible. The tendency is for the work to be allocated to more senior levels. You also need insights into the types of cases, the types of activities to deliver those case types, and the required skill levels.

This is where people analytics is critical. It gives you insights into how to resource a case – specifically the mix / balance between partners and junior lawyers, with effective delegation of activities where possible. This also helps balance workload across the team, prevents bottlenecks, and maximizes the billable potential.

Firms that are good at this also use this data for decisions around their talent pipeline – they can make sure they have the right number of people at the right levels to maximize profitability across all their cases.

Tailoring pricing to client needs and value perception

Data-driven / data-informed pricing requires insights into the relationship between the firm and each key client. These insights will also identify the clients who would benefit from AFA arrangements.

Analyzing client-specific data, such as retention rates, engagement patterns, Net Promoter Scores (i.e. satisfaction levels), and trends in payment history, provides a rich understanding of client behavior and preferences. This allows for the refinement of service offerings, tailoring of communication styles, and development of the most relevant pricing structures for the client.

Segmenting clients based on criteria such as industry / sector, case type, and case volume allows you to develop more targeted service packages and pricing models. Insights into your most valuable clients will allow you to focus resources on cultivating those client relationships.

This exercise is not just about internal financial data. It requires engaging with clients to understand their perceptions of value and their business objectives.

Cautions

Whilst historical data is a valuable source of insights, its limitations must be acknowledged and mitigated. Raw billing data, without the context regarding case scope, complexity, or outcomes, provides an incomplete and potentially misleading picture, making it virtually useless for precise future predictions. Without this contextual layer, comparing costs across cases or forecasting future expenses on historic data alone risks material inaccuracies. Therefore, effective analysis requires a richer data set that captures this context. This may require the implementation of more structured time recording practices to capture the required data. Increasingly, AI can be used to mine narratives to cluster, classify, and infer the nature and complexity of the work.

Pricing for uncertainty – the quantitative techniques

One of the hardest challenges in legal pricing is handling cases with inherent uncertainty, especially complex litigation, investigations, or transactional work where the scope can change rapidly. As mentioned above, there are flaws with using historical data alone. In this section, we will discuss some of the quantitative techniques that we can use to model and manage this uncertainty.

Data driven methodologies:

- *Predictive analytics.* This uses statistical algorithms and machine learning (ML) techniques to learn from history and predict future outcomes. For legal pricing applications, this includes predicting the duration of a case, estimating overall costs, and forecasting the probability of scenarios and outcomes (e.g. win via settlement vs trial). Whilst these predictions are not infallible, they provide grounding for more accurate initial quotes and managing client expectations.
- *Simulation (e.g. Monte Carlo).* Simulation models the potential impact or risk of key variables (costs, duration of tasks, probability of certain events). With the amount of computer power available, we can run thousands if not millions of simulations to generate a probability distribution of all possible outcomes (e.g. matter cost) rather than a single point estimate.
- *Scenario planning.* "What if?" analysis is performed on several potential scenarios. You can plan ahead for these scenarios occurring, understand the implications of each, and simulate the outcome – for example, staffing levels, rates, task durations, or even potential litigation pathways.
- *Decision analysis / decision trees.* These are structured logical approaches for mapping complex decisions under uncertainty. A decision tree visually represents the choices available (e.g. settle now vs proceed to trial), the potential uncertain events that could follow (e.g. motion granted, unfavorable verdict), the probabilities associated with these events, and the ultimate payoffs / costs of each branch. This helps quantify the potential benefits and costs of each option, and allows an informed decision on litigation strategies.
- *Phased pricing / structured AFAs.* Even when the scope is highly uncertain, the case can be broken down into more predictable phases. Fixed / capped fees can be applied to each of these phases to provide more predictability and control. You will have to include "material devia-

tions" as part of this pricing discussion with the client, and then maintain clear and regular communications throughout the phases. This is what is known as "risk collars".

Complementing the above methodologies, several quantitative methods can be used to incorporate risk into pricing models, including Quantitative Risk Analysis (QRA), Single Point Profitability Analysis, and Cost Realism Analysis.

Ultimately, we have to keep in mind that we are aiming to be "nearly right", not "precisely wrong". There is always uncertainty, which makes predicting the future hard. However, by using a greater range of these methodologies and quantitative techniques, we can make informed decisions based on the information we have available.

Negotiations with the client must include a clear articulation of these risks and their value. As a result, this becomes less about coming up with an exact number, and more about building in a series of trigger points over the lifecycle of a case that provide an opportunity to adjust the price or change the scope of work.

As we progress through a case, it is important to keep reviewing assumptions and maintaining clear communication with the client, especially when a material impact on the outcome emerges. This ensures alignment and allows collaboration with the client to navigate the uncertainties.

Building the analytics stack

So far, we have covered why analytics is important in legal pricing and the methods we use. This section is how we make the magic happen. This is about the technology stack that is used to perform the analytics.

At the most basic level:

- Plan what data you need.
- Capture data.
- Make the data usable.
- Perform calculations.
- Calculate a set of prices.

There are three core application types that are critical to a legal services firm. The first is a practice management system (PMS). This is the backbone. It provides the capability to:

- Open new cases.
- Record chargeable hours.

- Manage cases and workflows.
- Manage client monies (trust accounting) and pay disbursements.
- Generate bills from chargeable hours.
- Collect and allocation client receipts.
- Manage the firm financials.

The PMS is a transactional platform. It is used to manage transactional workflows. It is not good at reporting and analytics.

The second most important group of applications is what is collectively known as Business Intelligence (BI). This provides the capability to extract data, store data, aggregate and analyze insights, and create reporting. BI platforms are made up of multiple components. Firms can opt for an "all-in-one" BI provider, although it is increasingly common for a multi-vendor "stack". The latter provides more capability / agility through a best of breed product selection.

Lastly, there is document management (DMS). The ability to store, index, track, and retrieve any information relating to a case is a fundamental aspect of a lawyer's work.

In addition, there are several other application types that bolt on to enhance capability. Some of these provide enhancement to the three platforms described above. For example, eDiscovery platforms are used to supercharge the analysis of documents within the DMS. Some provide completely new functionality, for example, pricing and matter budgeting applications. There is also a very large ecosystem of applications that enhance a specific feature, for example for client onboarding and time recording.

There are also platforms that are used by other business operations functions that contain useful data. HR systems will contain all data relating to fee earners (grade, post qualification experience, performance review outcomes). Client Relationship Management (CRM) systems will contain details of all client interactions and general client intelligence, including key contact information and any sentiment data.

The legal services firm will generate a huge amount of data. Some of it is structured through the PMS. This can be easily analyzed through BI platforms. However, most of it is unstructured and within the DMS and email servers. With the rise of first ML and now AI, it has become much easier to gain insights from unstructured data. This will include detecting patterns of data (through clustering and classification algorithms) and finding hidden correlations (e.g. between a selection of documents and time recording data to provide insights into task duration).

Back to the question – what does the stack look like? What is the system architecture? Figure 1 shows the typical components needed in the technology stack for pricing.

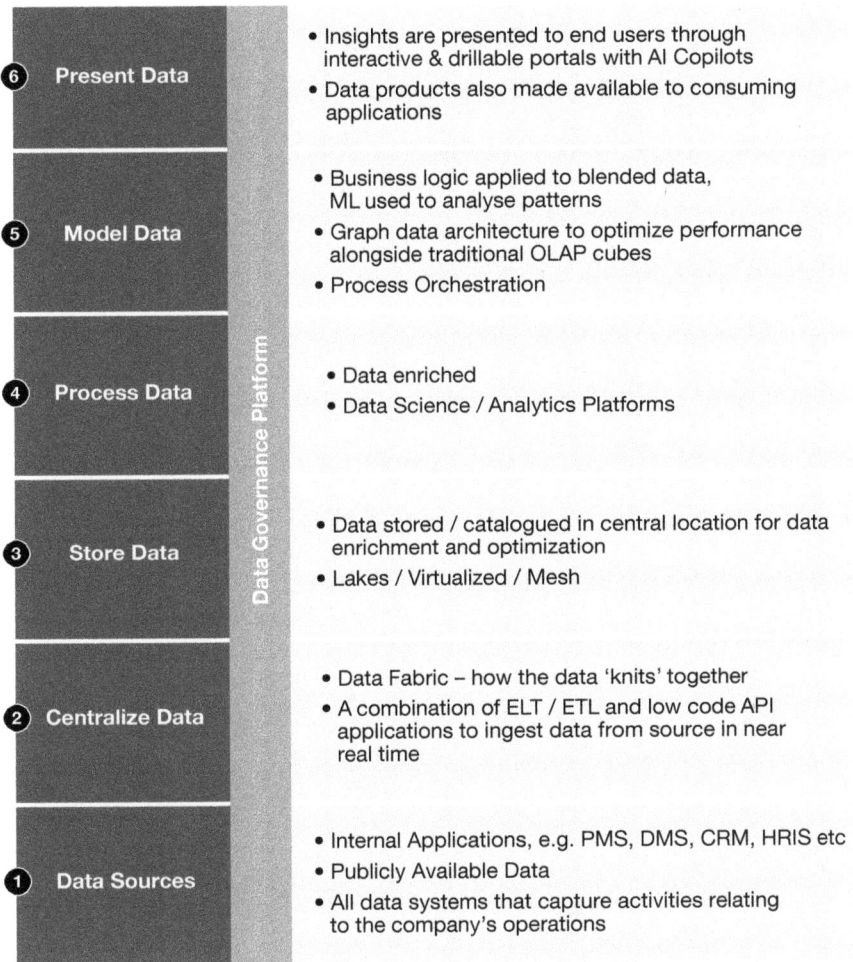

Step	Stage	Details
6	**Present Data**	• Insights are presented to end users through interactive & drillable portals with AI Copilots • Data products also made available to consuming applications
5	**Model Data**	• Business logic applied to blended data, ML used to analyse patterns • Graph data architecture to optimize performance alongside traditional OLAP cubes • Process Orchestration
4	**Process Data**	• Data enriched • Data Science / Analytics Platforms
3	**Store Data**	• Data stored / catalogued in central location for data enrichment and optimization • Lakes / Virtualized / Mesh
2	**Centralize Data**	• Data Fabric – how the data 'knits' together • A combination of ELT / ETL and low code API applications to ingest data from source in near real time
1	**Data Sources**	• Internal Applications, e.g. PMS, DMS, CRM, HRIS etc • Publicly Available Data • All data systems that capture activities relating to the company's operations

(Data Governance Platform spans the stack)

Figure 1: The tech stack for pricing.

In this model, the bottom sections are for the technologists, the middle sections are for the data scientists, and the top sections are for the users.

Coincidentally, the architecture for modern BI is very similar. The same concepts apply, and the same techniques are needed to process the same data sources. The difference here is building out the specialized use cases for pricing needs:

- Historical data insights.
- Projections.
- Ability to input matter plans.
- Generate matter budgets.
- Creating an RFP / pricing proposal.

This can be done through development of in-house technologies, or the implementation of increasingly available specialist legal pricing applications.

The people side of pricing technology

Even the greatest system is completely useless if a partner does not use it. One of the godfathers of business analytics, Professor Thomas Davenport,[5] states that there are three elements to success in this sphere:

- Curating the data.
- Deploying the tech stack.
- Building a data culture.

The last one is critical. This is about leading the proverbial horse to water and convincing them that they need to drink it. There is a huge prize at the end if we get it right – according to McKinsey research, the organizations that manage this will outperform their peers by up to 25 percent on EBITDA (i.e. profitability).[6]

However, the people side is really hard – especially in legal services environments. Attorneys are not naturally drawn to the numbers. Some can't do it, while others simply won't do it. They need to break age-old habits. There is a mindset shift that is needed – from decisions based on instinct (intuition is merely a data science algorithm in the mind) to decisions based on data. It is the opinion of this author that technology change needs to evolve at the same speed as the technology initiatives – a balanced evolution.[7]

Going too slow with tech will lead to frustration on the front line. Going too fast will lead to underutilization of the tech. Therefore, a huge amount of effort needs to be expended on building a data culture and data literacy within the fee earner community.

Achieving the culture change needed is an academic discipline in its own right. Here are eight "nudges" you can deploy to make it happen:

Analytics Technology Capability

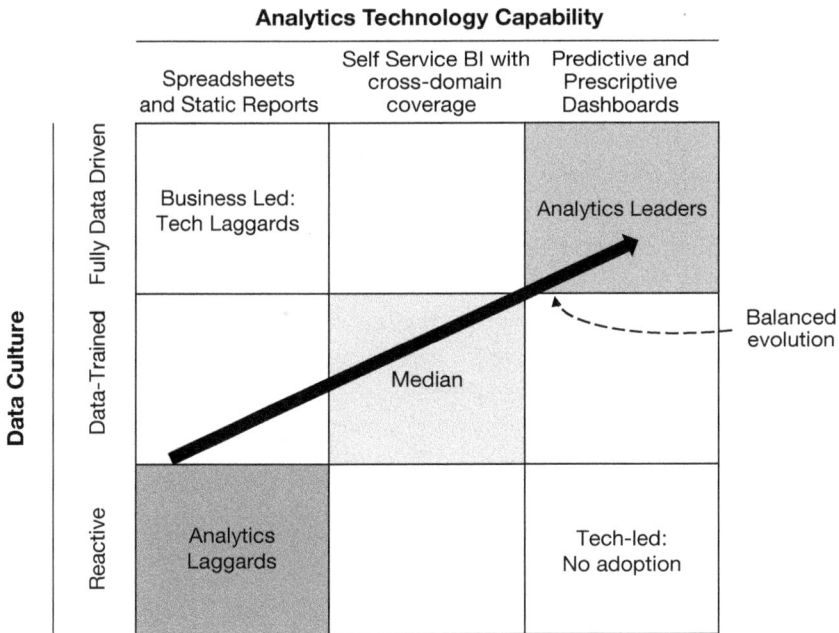

Figure 2: Tech vs data literacy maturity matrix.

1. Create a new KPI. Of the key pricing decisions, what percentage can be supported with analytics?
2. Emphasize the message from the top. "We must become data-driven, it is how we will achieve our strategic objectives."
3. Embed the requirement for validated reports (not Excel) as part of the risk policy.
4. Cascade the need for data-driven decisions as part of HR performance reviews.
5. When hiring, look for curious minds who will ask questions and demand analytics.
6. Provide training on data literacy for all lawyers.
7. Ensure that a link to personalized dashboards is on everyone's desktop or home screen.
8. Create analytical pathways for key decisions, guiding the user through the steps required for each decision and then pointing them toward the data to help make it.

Measuring performance and profitability

The legal profession attracts the brightest minds. These are also minds that need careful steering to ensure that everyone is working towards organizational objectives. This is where performance measures play a crucial role. If people are set a target, they will work towards it.

Unfortunately, in legal services, the metrics tend to relate to billable hours, not profitability. This skews behavior as a result. For example, it encourages time dumping, it disincentivizes delegation, and, most importantly, fee earners have no incentive to work at the maximum possible rate.

To define the metrics that drive more congruent behavior, you need to think about what you want people to do:

- Optimize pricing.
- Maximize case / matter profitability.
- Collect cash.
- Achieve client outcomes.

The key metrics to measure performance are as follows:

- Optimize pricing:
  - Client conversion percentage (in particular where price is cited as a reason).
  - Percent discount off rate card – with prior approval.
  - Percent discount off rate card – without prior approval.
- Case / matter profitability:
  - Write off percentage.
  - Realized rate per hour and realized profit per hour.
  - Activity cost vs budget.
- Collect cash:
  - Billing effectiveness percentage (i.e. percentage of WIP that has been billed).
  - Collections effectiveness percentage (i.e. percentage of bills that have been collected).
  - Lock up days.
- Achieve client outcomes
  - Case / matter outcome.
  - Net Promoter Score (i.e. client satisfaction).

Into the AI-enabled future

In 2024, over 80 percent of Fortune 500 CEOs cited Generative AI in their earnings calls.[8] It has clearly created a lot of hype. It has forced a mindset shift towards technology. Where technology was once underinvested in, Board level discussions are focused on how they can avoid getting left behind by competitors who make greater use of technology.

On the one hand, this is great from the perspective of evangelists who have been advocating for the increased use of technology within the legal sector, and its transformative potential. The downside is that not everyone truly understands AI. In this section we will explore areas where AI will enhance legal pricing with the caveat that this is still a rapidly evolving space and new use cases are emerging on an hourly basis.

Whilst the discussion of AI technologies is beyond the scope of this book, we will clarify three core areas:

1. *Machine learning (ML)* – a blanket term for mathematical techniques and algorithms that analyze trends and patterns within data, and learn from them to create predictions in new scenarios.

2. *Artificial intelligence (AI)* – used to learn and perform discrete tasks. Like ML, this is heavily based on mathematics and algorithms.

3. *Generative AI (GenAI)* – uses Large Language Models and is used to generate content.

We make this distinction because, in many use cases, traditional AI performs the analysis, whereas it is GenAI that creates the output documentation.

Refining pricing models

AI excels at analyzing vast and complex data sets. It can uncover patterns and trends that are missed by human analysts. These insights can be used to refine pricing models

Predictive power for forecasting client costs, possible duration, and outcomes

ML can analyze numerous data sets such as historical case data, specific case facts, jurisdictional trends, judge profiles, and even track records of opposing law firms. AI systems can then generate forecasts on a range of factors that influence pricing and strategy.

AI forecasts can be used to develop more accurate initial quotes and budgets. They can help manage client expectations early on, and they can help inform critical decisions. These forecasts can also help with allocating team resources based on the predicted complexity of the tasks involved in delivering the case. Risk assessments can also be turbo-charged as AI agents can research the impact of a greater number of potential risks.

Streamline operations

Robotic Process Automation (RPA) has been around a long time, and has been used for automating "If this, then that" rules-based tasks. These include retrieving and reviewing bank statements, retrieving information from external websites (e.g. land registry), and general administrative tasks.

However, RPA falls short where there is variability in the way these tasks are carried out. AI agents are now stepping in. Like RPA, they can automate routine tasks, but they have the ability to learn and react to variables. Example use cases include:

- Researching case precedents and statutes and building arguments.
- Increasing efficiency and effectiveness of eDiscovery by building chronologies, summarizing narratives, and identifying inconsistencies.
- In M&A transactions, AI agents can conduct due diligence by analyzing large volumes of documents and extracting critical information, identifying financial liabilities, and highlighting possible operational risks.
- For compliance, AI agents can continually monitor changes in regulations and ensure documents and practices adhere to the most recent standards.

Shifting the basis of the pricing model

We will not get away from thinking in terms of the billable hour. Even if we price differently, our costs are based on the capacity of fee earners. Therefore, to maximize profit, not only do we have to maximize price, we also have to maximize utilization.

Earlier in this chapter, we discussed that lawyers are disincentivized to become more efficient as they can't bill their time savings within the traditional model. However, as we can now closely predict the time taken for a task and how much the client values that task, we can more accurately assign a price / cost to that task. For example, let's say drafting a contract document takes five hours. We can set a "task" price based on five hours for the client. We can automate the generation of the document with AI and save four hours. This creates efficiencies, maintains pricing, and creates more capacity among the fee earner pool.

Challenges with AI – accuracy, hallucinations, and the black box

Despite the amazing AI capabilities we now have, it is not immune to errors, and we are seeing a lot of examples of "hallucinations". This is where AI models generate plausible-sounding but factually incorrect information. There have been instances of lawyers submitting legal briefs citing fictional AI-generated cases.[9]

This inherent issue means that you still need an eagle-eyed lawyer to perform rigorous review and verification of the outputs. The biggest barrier to date has been the adoption of AI. Stories about hallucinations do not help overcome this barrier, especially among a professional group known for its skepticism. One of the main reasons that this adoption barrier exists is because we cannot see what the AI is doing. It takes a set of instructions and returns the output. This makes it hard to verify – especially when analyzing large quantities of data. To overcome this, "explainability" needs to be built into AI workflows to allow for transparency and verification of the logic / rationale used.

Conclusions

Even with existing technologies, we have immense potential to transform the way we price with analytics and AI. This technology is improving at a rapid rate. It is essential for us to adopt these new technologies or get left behind. In particular, the tech makes AFAs and value-based pricing models more feasible.

We expect to see a gradual decline of the billable hour model. I know we've been saying this for years, but the right conditions are now in place. As AI adoption accelerates, time-based approaches to pricing will become less practical. In conjunction with persistent client demand, more firms will adopt AFAs.

What about the sophistication of pricing models? In the medium-term, we expect to see fixed fees dominate the AFA space. However, as AI starts to provide a far deeper understanding of case dynamics alongside client objectives, we will see more sophisticated AFA structures emerge. We will be able to price them profitably and effectively manage delivery against pre-agreed value metrics.

This will be underpinned by data analytics and AI, which will better equip firms to make more informed choices about their pricing models.

As the pace of technology increases, success is not just dependent on new technologies and new methods. It requires a fundamental mindset shift amongst the entire firm. Data analytics needs to be viewed as a strategic asset. We need to continue to invest in skills to leverage these tools. We need to foster a culture of data literacy.

Most importantly, we need to issue that call to action from the very top. The world really is changing – if we don't do this, we will get left behind.

References

1   LHH: Billable Hour vs AFAs: What's Right for Your Law Firm? www.lhh.com/en-us/insights/legal/billable-hour-vs-alternative-fee

2   Brightflag: Alternative Fee Arrangements Explained (Examples and Suggestions): https://brightflag.com/resources/alternative-fee-arrangements-examples/

3   Clio: AI-powered legal practices surge: Clio's latest Legal Trends Report reveals major shift: www.clio.com/about/press/clio-latest-legal-trends-report/

4   McKinsey: The Hidden Power of Pricing: www.mckinsey.com/capabilities/growth-marketing-and-sales/our-insights/ebook-the-hidden-power-of-pricing-how-b2b-companies-can-unlock-profit#/

5   https://en.wikipedia.org/wiki/Thomas_H._Davenport

6   McKinsey: Insights to impact: Creating and sustaining data-driven commercial growth: www.mckinsey.com/capabilities/growth-marketing-and-sales/our-insights/insights-to-impact-creating-and-sustaining-data-driven-commercial-growth

7   FP&A Trends: Mastering Data in FP&A: https://fpa-trends.com/sites/default/files/docs/FPA-Trends-Insights-Paper-2024-Mastering-Data-In-FPA.pdf

8   The AI Index 2024 Annual Report, Stanford University: https://hai.stanford.edu/ai-index/2024-ai-index-report

9   HAI: AI on Trial: Legal Models Hallucinate 1 out of 6 benchmarking queries: https://hai.stanford.edu/news/ai-trial-legal-models-hallucinate-1-out-6-or-more-benchmarking-queries

Chapter 6:

Behavioral economics and legal pricing – understanding client psychology

By Richard Burcher, founder and managing director, Validatum®, and founder and CEO, Virtual Pricing Director®

Pricing as psychology, not just arithmetic

The traditional view of legal pricing has been rooted in quantification – hours multiplied by rates, augmented by overheads and margins, and justified by complexity and expertise. While this approach may be operationally convenient for law firms, it fundamentally ignores the psychological journey clients undertake when evaluating a fee. Pricing, in truth, is not just a financial proposition – it is a cognitive, emotional, and relational experience.

Clients seldom evaluate price in isolation. They judge it through the lens of expectations, context, comparisons, and emotion. A fee that feels entirely reasonable in one situation may trigger discomfort or resistance in another – not because of a change in value, but because of a shift in perception.

This is where behavioral economics enters the frame. It challenges the notion that clients are rational calculators of cost and benefit. Instead, it paints a far more nuanced picture – clients rely on mental shortcuts, are susceptible to biases, and frequently make decisions that appear illogical when viewed through a purely economic lens but are perfectly coherent in psychological terms.

For law firm partners, this insight demands a paradigm shift. Effective pricing is not merely about arriving at a commercially sound number – it is about crafting a pricing experience that clients perceive as fair, proportionate, and aligned with their interests. Pricing becomes a strategic function, not an administrative task, a moment of persuasion, not a point of friction. Behavioral economics offers the tools to navigate this new terrain.

Behavioral economics – a primer for legal professionals

To apply behavioral economics to legal pricing, one must first understand its foundations. At its core, behavioral economics integrates insights from cognitive psychology with classical economic theory, acknowledging that real-world decision-making rarely conforms to the hyper-rational, utility-maximizing models found in textbooks.

System 1 and System 2 thinking

Nobel laureate Daniel Kahneman famously distinguished between two modes of thinking:

- *System 1:* Fast, automatic, instinctive, and emotionally charged. This is the system at play when a client glances at a proposal and instantly thinks, "That seems expensive".
- *System 2:* Slow, deliberative, logical, and effortful. This system is engaged when the client later dissects the proposal, compares it with alternatives, and asks probing questions.

The key insight is this – initial client reactions to price are often governed by System 1. First impressions, gut feelings, and emotional cues dominate. System 2 may enter the scene later, but by then, the pricing perception has already been framed. The early moments of exposure to a proposal are disproportionately influential.

Key biases and heuristics in legal pricing

Several cognitive biases are especially relevant to legal pricing:

- *Anchoring.* The first number a client sees (whether in a proposal or an informal discussion) sets a mental benchmark. All subsequent numbers are judged relative to it, even if the original figure is arbitrary. For example, if a client hears that "top-tier firms charge £500,000 for similar work", a £300,000 proposal may appear reasonable, even if the work could have been done for half that. Conversely, anchoring too low can undercut perceived value.
- *Loss aversion.* Clients experience the pain of losing a dollar more intensely than the pleasure of gaining one. This creates resistance to fee increases or scope changes, even when logically justified. It also means that reframing pricing to emphasize value preserved or risk avoided can be more persuasive than highlighting potential gains.
- *Framing effect.* The way information is presented affects interpretation. Saying "This work will cost £100,000" sounds heavier than "This investment secures comprehensive risk mitigation for less than 0.1 percent of the transaction value". Though the numbers are identical, the frames are not.

- *Availability bias.* Clients often rely on salient past experiences – whether with your firm or another – to judge current proposals. A single painful fee experience may color all future assessments, even if the context is entirely different.

By internalizing these biases, legal professionals can design pricing conversations and documentation that guide clients towards more favorable and constructive evaluations.

Understanding the client mindset

One of the most persistent errors law firms make is assuming that clients evaluate price through a rational, cost–benefit framework. While some clients (particularly procurement departments) may lean towards this, most decision-makers in legal services – GCs, CFOs, managing directors – engage in a far more complex cognitive process when assessing value.

Reference pricing and anchoring

Every client approaches a pricing conversation with a "reference price" in mind. This reference may stem from:
- Their last similar legal matter.
- Informal benchmarking from peers.
- Fees quoted by other firms.
- Internal budget constraints.
- Published legal pricing indices or surveys.

These anchors, however arbitrary, become the mental baseline. A proposed fee that exceeds this reference is automatically viewed as expensive, even if the scope or complexity justifies it. Likewise, a fee that falls below the anchor may be seen as suspiciously low, raising concerns about competence, resourcing, or completeness.

It's vital for partners to understand and, where possible, shape the client's reference point early. Dropping a premium anchor during scoping conversations – "This kind of matter often runs to £300,000 at the Magic Circle/AmLaw 25 level" – can condition clients to view your later £180,000 proposal as fair, even attractive.

Perceptions of fairness and process

Clients care deeply about how a fee is derived, not just what the number is.

The concept of procedural justice – a client's sense that the pricing process was transparent, consistent, and respectful – strongly affects their willingness to accept the outcome.

A fee presented without explanation feels arbitrary. A fee explained with reference to complexity, expected value, risk, and comparative benchmarks feels deliberate. Even if the latter is higher, clients are more likely to accept it.

This principle extends to scope changes and contingency planning. If clients are forewarned about the possibility of additional costs, and these are framed as fair responses to specific events, they are much less likely to object when the moment arises.

Trust, risk, and emotional security
Legal services are anxiety-laden purchases. Clients often feel exposed – legally, reputationally, and financially. A pricing conversation is not just a discussion about money – it is a moment where the client gauges whether they trust you, whether they feel understood, and whether they believe you will protect their interests.

A fee that feels out of step with the relationship or devoid of empathy can shatter that trust. Conversely, a transparent and consultative pricing approach can reinforce credibility, authority, and partnership.

Lawyers must understand that for most clients, price is not the problem – uncertainty is. The less ambiguity you leave in the pricing process, the more confident the client will feel in moving forward.

The psychology of fee structures
While much attention is paid to the amount charged, equal care must be given to the format in which that charge is delivered. The structure of a fee communicates powerful psychological messages about fairness, alignment, and risk allocation.

Hourly billing – familiar but flawed
The hourly rate remains dominant across much of the profession, but from a behavioral perspective, it is riddled with pitfalls:
- *It externalizes inefficiency.* Clients pay more when things take longer, even if the cause is internal to the firm.
- *It induces anxiety.* Every billable hour recorded feels like a new cost, activating the client's sense of loss repeatedly over the matter's duration.

- *It limits perceived control.* Clients cannot predict the total cost, which breeds distrust and budgetary discomfort.

From a psychological standpoint, hourly billing maximizes the pain of paying – the emotional discomfort of seeing fees accumulate without a clear endpoint.

Fixed and capped fees – buying certainty

Fixed and capped fees, by contrast, offer a sense of containment. Behavioral economics tells us that people are willing to pay a premium for certainty – particularly in anxiety-inducing contexts. A client may prefer a £200,000 fixed fee over a £150,000 estimate with open-ended potential, simply because the former removes ambiguity.

The preference is not always for the lowest fee but for the most predictable one. A fixed fee signals professionalism, planning, and alignment. However, it must be accompanied by clearly articulated scope boundaries and change protocols, or it may backfire when assumptions are breached.

Risk-sharing and success-based models

Alternative fee arrangements that link part of the firm's remuneration to outcomes are attractive for several behavioral reasons:

- They demonstrate confidence in the firm's ability to deliver.
- They signal alignment of incentives.
- They reduce the client's perceived exposure to downside risk.

However, such arrangements require precise definitions of success, credible measurement mechanisms, and thoughtful caps to prevent unbounded upside or perverse incentives.

In each of these structures, the key is not just what the fee is, but what it means. Clients interpret pricing formats as indicators of fairness, trust, and alignment. The chosen structure must support – not undermine – the broader narrative of partnership.

Choice architecture in legal pricing

Choice architecture refers to the deliberate structuring of how options are presented to influence decision-making. In legal pricing, this is far more than a cosmetic consideration. How you frame the client's options directly affects which one they choose, how they feel about it afterwards, and whether they perceive the process as empowering or overwhelming.

Why binary choices are risky

Many law firms present pricing in binary form: "Here is our fee. Please let us know." This approach may feel decisive, but it actually creates tension. It frames the proposal as a yes-or-no proposition, forcing the client into an evaluative posture rather than a collaborative one. Behaviorally, it encourages objection or negotiation rather than engagement.

By contrast, offering a menu of options – with meaningful differences in scope, risk allocation, or level of service – invites the client into a position of agency. They are no longer asking, "Do I accept this price?" but "Which of these approaches best suits my needs?". That subtle shift in framing increases conversion rates and satisfaction.

The decoy effect and strategic anchoring

The decoy effect occurs when the introduction of a third, less attractive option changes how people evaluate two others. Consider three options:
- Option A: £60,000 – core scope only.
- Option B: £90,000 – core + advisory + risk assessment.
- Option C: £95,000 – same as B with redundant extras.

Option C makes Option B look more reasonable and well-rounded. Most clients will avoid the extreme (Option C) and the bare minimum (Option A) in favor of the "sensible middle". Importantly, Option B is the one you want them to choose. The decoy is not dishonest – it's a way to structure preferences based on client psychology.

Goldilocks pricing and the power of three

The principle of Goldilocks pricing – offering three choices (basic, standard, premium) – leverages a powerful behavioral tendency. People avoid extremes and gravitate towards the center. When structured properly, this approach allows you to:
- Showcase your full capabilities (premium).
- Demonstrate price sensitivity (basic).
- Steer clients toward the most commercially desirable option (standard).

The key is ensuring that each tier is credible, differentiated, and justifiable. The standard option should represent the best balance of comprehensiveness and cost-effectiveness.

Avoiding the paradox of choice

While options empower clients, too many can paralyze them. This is known as the paradox of choice – when overwhelmed by alternatives, people become anxious, defer decisions, or default to the safest (often cheapest) option.

Limit the proposal to three clearly framed options, each with a distinct rationale and outcome. Supplement this with a table or matrix comparing features and benefits, using client-centric language like "best suited for those who want...".

Great pricing is not about the hard sell. It is about curating a set of choices that allow the client to align price, value, and risk in a way that feels deliberate and reassuring.

Framing and narrative in price communication

Framing refers to the context in which a message is delivered and the language used to express it. In legal pricing, the difference between acceptance and resistance often hinges less on the actual fee than on how it is presented.

The power of contextual anchors

A £200,000 fee for a legal matter may seem high – until it's presented next to the £20 million value of the transaction it supports. Similarly, a retainer of £10,000/month may feel steep, unless reframed as "equivalent to the salary of one mid-level in-house counsel, but with access to a full team of specialists".

Clients rely on these comparisons to make sense of unfamiliar numbers. Providing them proactively is not manipulative – it is supportive. You are helping the client understand where your fee sits relative to value created, risk mitigated, or alternatives considered.

Positive vs negative framing

Behavioral studies show that people respond very differently to gains and losses, even when the underlying facts are the same. For example:
- *Positive frame:* "If you instruct us this month, we can offer a ten percent early commitment discount".
- *Negative frame:* "A ten percent surcharge applies to engagements commencing after this month".

Clients are far more receptive to gaining a benefit than avoiding a penalty.

Therefore, frame adjustments or incentives in terms of benefits received, not costs avoided.

Breaking down the whole
Fees are often perceived as more palatable when broken into smaller components:
- £300,000 over a year becomes £25,000/month.
- A fixed fee of £75,000 can be framed as "equivalent to £2,500 per day over a month of intensive legal support".

This temporal framing reduces cognitive friction. It also allows clients to align your fee with internal budgeting cycles or cost structures they understand – such as staff salaries or project costs.

Telling the price story
Narrative is a powerful cognitive tool. Instead of stating, "Our fee is £100,000," say:

"To provide strategic advisory, due diligence, and regulatory compliance on this £35 million acquisition, our fixed fee is £100,000. This includes a cross-practice team of senior specialists, rapid turnaround for board materials, and post-deal integration support."

This narrative:
- Reframes the fee as an investment rather than an expense.
- Connects price to outcomes and value.
- Demonstrates proactive planning and control.

In short, every price has a story, and partners must learn to tell it effectively. Clients are not comparing your price to perfection – they are comparing it to the alternatives you help them visualize.

The psychology of discounts and concessions
Discounting is ubiquitous in legal pricing. But it is often applied reactively, driven by discomfort, perceived competitive pressure, or a desire to "get the deal over the line". From a behavioral perspective, this is dangerous territory.

How discounts erode value perception
Clients interpret discounts as signals. When a 20 percent reduction is offered without resistance or explanation, clients infer that:

- The original fee was inflated.
- The firm is insecure or desperate.
- The real value is lower than presented.

This undermines trust and undermines the brand of the firm, the practice group, and the individual partner. Worse, it anchors the client's sense of your value at the discounted level. The next time you quote full price, it feels like a loss, triggering resistance.

Discount addiction and escalation
Once a discount has been received, behavioral consistency kicks in. Clients expect it again. If another partner in your firm later proposes standard pricing, the client feels penalized. They perceive inconsistency, arbitrariness, and a breach of precedent.

Over time, this dynamic creates discount escalation – clients not only expect reductions, they begin demanding deeper ones. Law firms that indulge in unstructured discounting often find themselves chasing margin erosion with volume – a vicious and counter-productive cycle.

Strategic alternatives to discounting
Rather than reduce fees, consider these behaviorally sound alternatives:
- *Conditional concessions.* Offer a discount only if certain conditions are met (e.g., decision by a certain date, longer-term commitment, or immediate payment terms). This reframes the discount as a reward, not a default.
- *Value-added extras.* Include a minor service at no additional cost, such as a post-transaction debrief or quarterly compliance update. Clients perceive this as generous rather than transactional.
- *Scope reduction.* Adjust the deliverables. Rather than cutting the price by 15 percent, reduce the scope by 15 percent and hold your rate. This protects value perception while being responsive.
- *Fee staging.* Spread the fee into instalments aligned with milestones. This does not reduce the fee but makes it feel more manageable.

In all cases, the principle is the same. Don't discount to appease – offer alternatives that preserve value and create reciprocity.

Client behavioral segmentation

Not all clients think alike. Applying a single pricing strategy to every client ignores the diversity of cognitive styles, risk profiles, and emotional drivers that influence legal buying decisions.

Behavioral segmentation allows law firms to tailor pricing approaches to different psychological archetypes. This improves client comfort, alignment, and engagement.

The Analytical Evaluator
- *Traits:* Data-driven, process-oriented, often from finance or procurement backgrounds.
- *Behaviors:* Request detailed breakdowns, ask for benchmarking data, challenge assumptions.
- *Best approach:* Present itemized proposals, include ROI or efficiency arguments, show comparators or historical data.

The Relational Collaborator
- *Traits:* Values trust, rapport, and shared history over technical detail.
- *Behaviors:* Responds to tone, warmth, and signs of partnership. Less concerned with price precision.
- *Best approach:* Frame price in terms of long-term relationship and support. Emphasize dependability and responsiveness.

The Risk-Averse Steward
- *Traits:* Concerned with predictability, reputation risk, and accountability.
- *Behaviors:* Avoids open-ended fees, asks about contingencies, prefers clear contracts.
- *Best approach:* Offer fixed or capped fees, clearly define scope, explain risk mitigation strategies.

The Outcome-Focused Executive
- *Traits:* Results-oriented, impatient with detail, makes decisions quickly.
- *Behaviors:* Asks "What's the result?", not "What's the process?". Ignores line items; focuses on impact.
- *Best approach:* Highlight deliverables, outcomes, and success metrics. Propose performance-linked fees or retainers.

Understanding these behavioral types enables lawyers to shift from rigid pricing templates to bespoke pricing dialogues. It also builds empathy, which enhances trust and improves commercial outcomes.

Practical applications in pricing conversations

The concepts outlined in this chapter only come to life when deployed in conversation. A pricing model may be rational, elegant, and commercially sound, but it is the moment of presentation and discussion that determines its fate. This is where behavioral economics meets interpersonal skill.

Preparation – behavioral intelligence as strategic advantage

The most effective pricing conversations are never improvised. They are meticulously prepared in three dimensions:

1. *Client-specific behavioral analysis*. What type of decision-maker is this client? Analytical? Risk-averse? Status-driven? What biases might shape their response?
2. *Contextual anchoring*. What prior fee experiences, firm interactions, or market comparisons are likely influencing their expectations?
3. *Narrative alignment*. What story will make the proposal feel proportionate, predictable, and valuable?

Without this preparation, lawyers risk triggering cognitive resistance – surprise, distrust, sticker shock, or disengagement.

Behavioral techniques in live dialogue

Several techniques derived from behavioral science can be deployed in real time:

- *Anchoring high*. Open with a premium, fully featured option before introducing the one you wish them to choose. This sets the mental benchmark. Even if the client does not select it, it reframes the rest of the conversation.
- *Social proof*. Reference how other clients in similar sectors or matters chose certain fee structures. "Many of our clients in your industry opt for this approach because it gives them predictable cost exposure while allowing flexibility for scope shifts."
- *Narrative framing*. Rather than presenting the fee as a lump sum, contextualize it within the client's goals. "This represents about 0.2 percent of the transaction value and ensures 360-degree legal risk coverage during a critical phase."

- *Loss framing in decision deadlines.* Instead of saying, "We can hold this fee until Friday", say, "After Friday, this fee structure will no longer be available due to internal resource reallocation". This activates the client's aversion to loss and delay.
- *Reciprocity nudges.* Share a useful insight, resource, or early risk flag for free during the scoping stage. This small act builds trust and creates a subtle social contract, making the client more inclined to engage you.

Language and emotion regulation

Many partners overexplain when anxious. Longwinded fee justifications can sound defensive. Others err in the opposite direction – abruptly dropping a number without framing or rationale.

The behavioral sweet spot is calm confidence, conversational pacing, and emotionally intelligent framing. Signal that pricing is negotiable within boundaries, but not apologetically elastic. Clients respect confidence more than concessions.

Ultimately, a pricing conversation is not about "winning" or "defending" a fee. It is about creating shared understanding. The goal is not to avoid objection, but to anticipate and pre-empt it with clarity, empathy, and structure.

Embedding behavioral pricing in firm culture

Behavioral pricing cannot rely solely on the instincts of individual rainmakers. To be effective at scale, it must become part of the firm's cultural infrastructure – embedded in how pricing is trained, supported, and governed.

Partner enablement and pricing literacy

Most law firm partners are deeply skilled in law and client service, but less comfortable with pricing psychology. Few have formal training in behavioral economics or commercial negotiation.

Firms must address this by:
- *Developing pricing academies.* Ongoing professional development focused on behavioral strategy, scoping, communication, and fee design.
- *Simulated pricing scenarios.* Partners should rehearse pricing conversations in high-fidelity simulations. Roleplay builds muscle memory and desensitizes discomfort.
- *Sharing behavioral win stories.* Internal case studies of successful pricing conversations – especially those that overcame initial resistance – should be widely circulated to shift cultural norms.

- *Use the right software.* Solutions like Virtual Pricing Director® incorporate many of these concepts and, in so doing, go well beyond Excel and products that take the same one-dimensional arithmetical approach only.

Standardizing behaviorally intelligent templates

Pricing is often inconsistent across a firm. Some proposals are detailed and thoughtful – others feel rushed or opaque. Behavioral science can be embedded into template design to ensure consistency:

- Tiered pricing models as default.
- Language templates that include framing guidance.
- Visual aids that compare options in client-friendly ways.

These tools help less experienced partners adopt best practice without having to reinvent the wheel for each matter.

Again, solutions like Virtual Pricing Director® increasingly provide this capability.

Cross-functional collaboration

Behavioral pricing should not be siloed within partners or BD teams. It should involve:

- *Marketing:* To shape messaging and value propositions.
- *Finance:* To align behavioral tactics with profitability metrics and to monitor realization.
- *Client listening teams:* To harvest feedback about how pricing conversations are experienced and where misalignments occur.

This integrated approach builds institutional memory and continuous improvement.

Governance and post-mortems

Post-matter reviews should include a behavioral pricing debrief:

- Was the client's decision pattern anticipated accurately?
- Did the fee structure match their cognitive and emotional needs?
- What framing techniques worked – or fell flat?
- What should we replicate or refine?

In this way, pricing becomes a discipline, not a one-off performance.

Case studies and examples

The practical value of behavioral pricing is best illustrated through real-world examples. The following anonymized cases reflect firms that consciously applied behavioral principles – with measurable results.

Case 1: Transforming pitch conversion with tiered options

A leading European commercial firm moved from offering single-solution proposals to a three-tier pricing structure:
- Tier 1: Core deliverables, lowest fee.
- Tier 2: Standard package with advisory integration.
- Tier 3: Premium, including post-matter analysis and 24-hour response SLA.

Over a 12-month period:
- Proposal conversion increased by 28 percent.
- 64 percent of clients chose the middle tier.
- Fee disputes dropped significantly.

Clients reported that the tiered structure made them feel more in control and better able to calibrate service to budget.

Case 2: Strategic anchoring in regulatory advisory

An APAC boutique, bidding for a regulatory compliance retainer, framed its $180,000/year proposal next to benchmark figures from international firms ranging from $250,000 to $400,000. Although the client initially hesitated at the number, the anchoring repositioned the fee as good value rather than expensive.

The firm won the engagement without discounting – and retained it for three consecutive years.

Case 3: Replacing discount culture with value framing

A US mid-sized litigation practice discovered that its partners were routinely applying unstructured discounts of 15-25 percent to "secure" work. A pricing intervention program replaced discounting with:
- Conditional incentives (e.g., multi-matter packages).
- Fixed fee menus for the more predictable phases of litigation.
- Narrative training to better explain price logic.

Within six months:
- Average discounts dropped to under five percent.
- Partner confidence in pricing conversations rose markedly.
- Realization improved by 11 percent, with no reduction in client net promoter scores.

These examples underscore a core truth – behavioral pricing is not about gimmicks. It is about thoughtful, evidence-based client engagement.

Pricing as a strategic differentiator

Legal pricing is entering a new era – one defined less by hourly inputs and more by psychological intelligence, client experience, and strategic value communication. In this context, behavioral economics is not a luxury – it is a competitive necessity.

The firms that succeed will be those that:
- Understand client psychology as deeply as they understand the practice of law.
- Treat pricing not as a final act of sales, but as a central pillar of brand, trust, and differentiation.
- Train their people to speak the language of outcomes, not just deliverables.
- Move beyond reactive fee setting toward intentional, behaviorally grounded pricing architecture.

In doing so, they will achieve more than increased margins or improved conversion. They will redefine what it means to be client-centered – not by capitulating to pressure, but by architecting pricing experiences that feel fair, empowering, and value-rich.

Behavioral economics offers the legal profession a toolkit to do just that. Not in theory, but in every conversation, proposal, and engagement we undertake.

Chapter 7:
Transparency and trust in the legal industry

By Jack Kingston, account manager, BigHand

In today's legal market, clients continue to demand more transparency in their legal engagements. Gone are the days when clients were loyal to just one firm – now they shop around for the most competitive price and value on legal services. As a result, firms must be transparent about scoping and put more emphasis on the value they bring to the market. Firms, on the other hand, must protect their bottom line, while still delivering value to the clients. Alternate fee arrangements and fixed fees to mitigate write-offs and write-downs are a good strategy to safeguard profitability, especially as law firms drive efficiencies through AI. By leveraging the right people, processes, and technologies, firms can improve communication and even educate their clients on how to be savvy while they pursue legal engagements. In this chapter, I discuss how law firms can leverage relationships and transparency in pricing models to remain profitable in the ever-changing market.

Building trust

Attorneys are legally and ethically bound to act in their client's best interest. Many clients still feel vulnerable and uncertain when engaging with legal service providers. A major contributor to this discomfort is a lack of transparency, especially around costs, timing, and scope. This is where a pricing director comes in.

Some purchasers of legal services do not fully understand what legal services entail, how long they will take, or how much they will cost. The ones who do, such as a large legal department, are looking for clarity and value. This uncertainty leads to hesitation, fear of hidden fees, and a reluctance to engage legal counsel until necessary, or worse yet, shop for their legal services elsewhere. Corporate legal departments are keeping more work in-house and using AI to deliver this work, which means law firms have to work even harder to attract and retain customers. It's no longer the case that a client stays with one firm out of loyalty for a particular partner or because the firm was "their parents' lawyer".

Any law firm I speak with wants to serve its clients with honesty and clarity, much like I do as a vendor to the legal industry. But the traditional legal model, dominated by hourly rates, complex retainers, and ambiguous quotes, often gets in the way.

Is the billable hour getting in the way?

The billable hour has long been the foundation of the business model. While it may work for internal time tracking and cost allocation, it can create poor customer experience. Consider the typical client reaction to hourly billing:

"How many hours will this take?"

"Why did this cost more than expected?" ("And why am I only finding out at the end?")

"Who is working on this, and why?"

Hourly billing can muddy the waters on the actual cost of legal services until after the fact. Clients are unable to budget, compare, or predict total spending. They may also request "shadow billing" on a fixed-fee engagement, which can create inefficiencies and lead to lost time (leakage). More often than not, when overruns occur, they will ask for time to be written off or for additional discounts, both of which negatively impact the firm's profitability.

Transparency matters

In today's landscape, clients expect clarity and openness from all professionals they hire, from financial advisors to real estate agents. Legal services are no exception. Clients often have little understanding of the scope or the cost of the desired legal services, which in turn leads to scope misalignment, client frustrations, and leakage for the firm.

BigHand's Annual Law Firm Finance Report[1] ran a survey of over 800 law firm leaders in 2025 (see Figure 1). The data showed that clients are focused on financial transparency throughout the entire matter lifecycle:

- 85 percent of clients are demanding greater transparency during the life cycle of matter.
- 75 percent of clients are requesting more alternative fee arrangements (AFAs).
- 75 percent of firms expect an increase in write-offs and write-downs in the coming year.

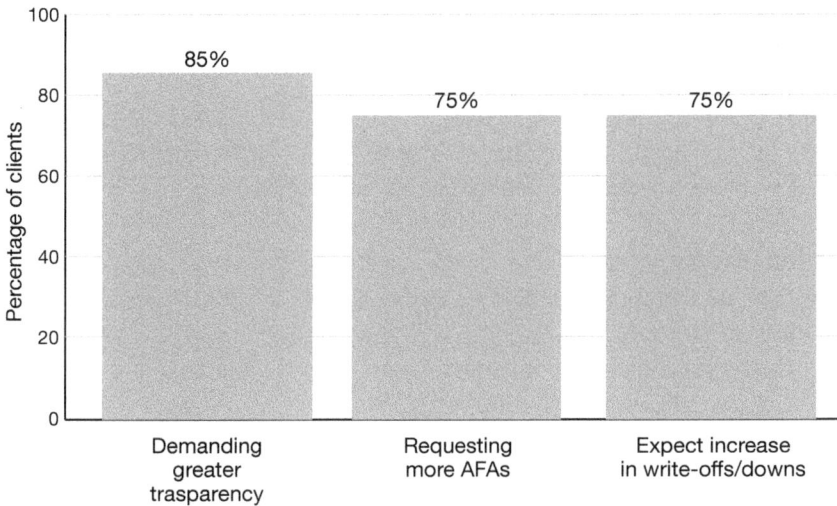

Figure 1: Client expectations in the legal industry. Source: BigHand.

Empowering clients and increasing collections

Transparency in the way matters are scoped and presented gives clients more control over their legal journey, or at least a perception of increased control and engagement. When they understand how the provider prices services, what outcomes are likely, and what costs are involved, they are more confident, engaged, and satisfied. A satisfied client is less likely to shop for their services elsewhere, leading to longer-lasting business relationships. They will also be more likely to pay their bills on time, reducing the need for a law firm to dip into a high-interest line of credit to keep operating effectively. We have seen a few firms in the North American market go under due to the higher costs of operation that result from the rising cost of borrowing, amongst other costs for running a firm.

Realization and increased collections for the law firm

If work is priced and planned properly, the firm is likely to increase realization and develop better collection habits. It's commonly known that for every 30-day increase in lock-up, the total amount that can be collected drops by about ten percent. Think about how many millions of dollars could be recovered simply by keeping a keen eye on the scope and by communicating with clients along the way.

The power of utilization

One of the major byproducts of a proper pricing strategy is better utilization of their legal resources. If partner time can shift downward to an associate, the cost of the matter for the client will decrease, without a firm losing out on any profits. Associates are the most profitable resources a firm can use, so why not have metrics around using them effectively?

Flat-fee services

Many legal matters lend themselves well to flat-fee pricing, including:

- Wills and trusts.
- Business creation and incorporation.
- Contract reviews or creation (with AI).
- Real estate.
- Trademark registrations.

Flat fees provide predictability for both the firm and the client. They reduce billing disputes, improve client satisfaction, and incentivize efficiency. A pricing director can leverage data from past matters, often using a leading pricing tool from a vendor to help increase visibility from similar engagements. Good data means a repeatable process that helps improve efficiency. In addition, law firms can easily utilize the value of AI for many of these tasks, making the matter even more profitable.

Communication and process

Transparency is not only limited to pricing engagements – it extends to the entire client experience. A pricing director coupled with a legal project manager can speak to clients on behalf of the partnership to explain the status of the engagement. They can stay out in front of scope changes or overages by scheduling recurring meetings with key stakeholders to deliver the ongoing scope of the work.

Clear scope of work

Legal services are complex, but clients should never be confused about what they are dishing out their hard-earned money for.

Spell out the scope of engagement, including:

- What is included?
- What is not included.
- Expected timeline.
- Roles and responsibilities.

This reduces misunderstandings, improves collaboration, and ensures alignment. The obvious windfall to the firm will be less leakage by way of write-offs and write-downs, which undermine law firm profitability.

Leveraging technology to improve client communication and transparency

In an increasingly competitive legal landscape, clients are demanding more than just high-quality legal work. They expect clarity, predictability, and fairness in pricing. For law firms, this shift has placed new importance on the role of the legal pricing director – a professional who bridges the gap between legal teams and clients by managing fee structures, budgets, and profitability. One of the core challenges in this role is communication, particularly when it comes to ensuring transparency around fees, scope, and value. Fortunately, technology is proving to be a powerful enabler for legal pricing directors, helping them build trust, reduce friction, and enhance client relationships. Having good pricing tools will also help a law firm attract top end talent to lead their pricing teams.

Data visualization tools – keeping it simple(r)

Legal pricing involves an array of variables, hourly rates, staffing models, historical performance, matter complexity, and client expectations. Communicating these intricacies to clients can be challenging, especially if the data resides in outdated spreadsheets or is presented in opaque formats.

Technology solves this with data visualization platforms. There are many tools on the market that allow pricing directors to turn raw data into intuitive charts and graphs. For example, rather than sending clients a table of rates and hours, a pricing director can present a visual breakdown of where time is incurred, how costs are allocated across phases, and what variables drive price adjustments. This makes it easier for clients to understand the rationale behind pricing models and gives them a sense of control and clarity.

Visual transparency also builds confidence. Clients are more likely to trust pricing when they can see historical data, market benchmarks, and performance metrics presented in an objective, digestible format. Moreover, law firms can leverage the same graphics to ensure their matters are on track and profitable, and to understand the "real" impact of a write-off, write-down, discount, or even changing the staffing models and shifting work downward to an associate when it makes sense. Remember, if you can see it, you can easily measure it, and if you can measure it you can act on it.

Predictability prevents pain

Budget overruns are a major source of client dissatisfaction. They often result from poor scoping, unexpected legal developments, or lack of real-time tracking, which can be mitigated by using data to plan a matter. A legal pricing director, armed with modern budgeting and forecasting tools, can change this dynamic entirely.

For clients, this level of foresight is incredibly valuable. It allows them to plan their internal payments and make informed decisions about the engagement. When engagements are presented as a dynamic, data-driven model rather than a static fee or hourly rate, it invites open and honest conversations about value.

These platforms also enable budget-to-actual tracking. A legal pricing director can set up alerts or dashboards that notify clients when spending is nearing budget thresholds, ensuring there are no surprises. This real-time visibility enhances transparency and accountability, reducing the tension that often accompanies billing discussions. It keeps the firm on track to work towards a meaningful engagement, which is paramount to staying profitable. Staying out in front of "cost overrun" discussions can drastically reduce the need to discount the matter or write off valuable time.

People, process, and technology

While technology can be an enabler, it will not be successful without the right people and processes in place to support it. A strong pricing director still needs to communicate, listen, and understand the needs of their customers. Technology will never replace the human element but enhance it. It is paramount that there are processes that lead to the success of a powerful pricing tool. Technology cannot solve the problem but it can make things much easier to achieve.

The evolution of the pricing director

At a recent conference I attended, the group spoke about how the pricing director role will continue to evolve. Beyond increased communication on behalf of the partnerships in areas like scope, addressed above, their duties will expand. One major area is helping current clients write RFPs so the client can gain more understanding of the engagement, while the firm can benefit from client retention with RFPs written for their in-house services. They will also need to show the client benefit from services generated via AI, as a current fear within the industry is how they will pass on AI fees to the client as the demand for certain services dwindles based on automation.

What about AI? Will it help or hinder communication?

While nobody can predict the future and how, AI will certainly play a part in your communication strategy. There are ways to get ahead of the curve. Numerous vendors have created products that embed AI to ensure that data is entered properly. To use the simple "garbage in, garbage out" analogy, if your data is in good condition, you can use it to drive an AI based structure. To get ready, firms should make sure that tasks are coded properly so they know what "really happened" to model future matters correctly. Existing AI platforms can be leveraged to help firms get ready for the new wave and increase communication in their existing environments. Keep data sanitized and your firm will thank you for it.

Conclusion

The landscape of the legal industry is shifting. Firms need to stay on top of client demands to remain profitable. Pricing directors will play a critical role in increased communication with clients and prospective clients alike. Having good processes in place, underpinned by technology, will allow firms to retain clients and even identify areas of cross-selling to their existing clients. Remember, it takes years to build a relationship, and only seconds to damage it. Taking care of your business will mean the business will take care of you and put more money in the hands of your partners.

References

1   www.bighand.com/en-gb/resources/whitepapers/annual-law-firm-finance-report-2025/

Chapter 8:
Fixed fees and predictability – meeting modern client demands

By Richard Burcher, founder and managing director, Validatum®, and founder and CEO, Virtual Pricing Director®

The predictability imperative

The legal industry is navigating a profound shift in the way clients perceive value. Once, the simple delivery of legal expertise was sufficient to justify a fee, regardless of its unpredictability. Today, this dynamic has been inverted. Clients no longer measure value solely in terms of competence – they now judge firms equally on transparency, efficiency, and predictability.

Hourly billing – long the default model – has increasingly come under fire. From a client perspective, this model seems structurally misaligned with their needs. It exposes them to financial risk by transferring all uncertainty onto their shoulders. When a matter overruns, the client pays for the inefficiency, delays, or miscalculations of their lawyers. As one general counsel put it bluntly, *"Hourly billing is the only business model in the world where a supplier earns more when they are less efficient".*

The modern business environment places extraordinary emphasis on financial discipline and predictability. General counsel and CFOs, often under direct pressure from boards and shareholders, require:

- Certainty of legal spend, especially for major projects and disputes.
- Transparency, with clear assumptions and deliverables.
- Alignment between price and value, rather than cost and time.

Fixed fees directly respond to these priorities. They provide clients with confidence and cost control, enabling them to plan effectively and avoid the discomfort of escalating invoices. Moreover, fixed fees convey that the firm is confident in its own processes, efficient in delivery, and aligned with the client's interests.

For law firms, the transition to fixed pricing is both challenging and rewarding. It demands greater scoping precision, data-driven planning, and operational discipline. But when properly implemented, fixed fees often strengthen client relationships, improve competitive positioning, and – contrary to some beliefs – can deliver higher profitability than traditional hourly models.

The evolution of client demands

The shift towards fixed fees is part of a broader evolution in how corporate clients procure professional services. Over the past two decades, clients have become more sophisticated, commercial, and cost-conscious in their approach to legal spend.

The rise of legal operations and procurement

In-house legal departments now resemble business units. They employ legal operations professionals who bring expertise in budgeting, metrics, and vendor management. These teams treat law firms not as exceptional advisors but as service providers to be measured against performance metrics and cost benchmarks.

Procurement teams are also playing a more assertive role. Their mandate is to drive value, negotiate competitive terms, and introduce pricing discipline. They challenge firms to provide:

- Clear fee proposals.
- Alternatives to hourly billing.
- Risk-sharing arrangements such as fixed or capped fees or outcome-based fees.

This procurement-led approach has forced firms to compete on factors beyond reputation and expertise. Pricing models are now a major differentiator.

Lessons from other professional services

The legal profession is not unique in facing this shift. The accounting industry, for example, adapted decades ago. Audits, tax filings, and compliance work are almost always performed under fixed or capped pricing. Similarly, IT consulting firms frequently use project-based pricing, reflecting defined deliverables and milestones.

Clients now ask why law firms – who claim to have unparalleled expertise – cannot provide similar certainty. For them, fixed pricing is a hallmark of a commercially mature supplier.

The end of tolerance for cost overruns
Ten years ago, a client might have grudgingly accepted an invoice that exceeded the initial estimate. Today, that same client is far more likely to challenge the bill or demand discounts. This is not simply about cost-cutting – it reflects a deeper expectation that suppliers own the financial risk of inefficiency.

For law firms, this is both a warning and an opportunity. Firms that master predictable pricing can turn it into a competitive advantage, while those clinging to hourly billing risk being sidelined.

Understanding predictability as client value
For clients, predictability is not a "nice-to-have". It is a form of value in its own right. A law firm that provides a clear, upfront price is seen as reliable, professional, and confident in its ability to deliver.

Ian McDougall, executive vice president and general counsel with LexisNexis says:

> *"I have conversations with law firms very often... and I'm sure they don't believe me when I say to them that we are after quality and not necessarily the cheapest one. We're after value for money. And one of the biggest elements of that is predictability. Can you give me a predictable cost?"*[1]

Predictability as risk mitigation
Uncertainty is a form of risk. For CFOs, unpredictable costs are viewed no differently from supply chain disruptions or currency fluctuations – they are variables that threaten financial stability. A fixed fee shifts some of this risk from the client to the firm. Even if the fixed fee is slightly higher than the expected hourly total, clients appreciate the certainty of no surprises.

Behavioral dynamics of predictability
Behavioral economics explains why predictability is so valued:
- *Loss aversion.* Clients feel the pain of unplanned cost overruns far more acutely than the pleasure of unexpected savings.
- *Cognitive load reduction.* A fixed fee simplifies decision-making. The client doesn't need to monitor every time entry or debate each incremental cost.
- *Trust signals.* A firm that confidently quotes a fixed fee signals operational mastery. It suggests that the firm understands the scope, has handled similar matters before, and can control its processes.

Clients paying a premium for certainty

It is a mistake to assume that clients want the cheapest price. In reality, they often prefer to pay slightly more for certainty. For instance, a general counsel might choose a £500,000 fixed fee over a £450,000 estimate because the latter involves risk of escalation. Predictability is a premium feature.

Predictability as relationship capital

Clients remember not only the quality of legal outcomes but also how they felt during the process. A predictable, transparent pricing model reduces anxiety and builds goodwill. Over time, this trust translates into repeat instructions, referrals, and stronger strategic partnerships.

Myths and misconceptions about fixed fees

Despite these advantages, many firms hesitate to embrace fixed fees, citing misconceptions that do not hold up under scrutiny.

Myth 1: Fixed fees are less profitable

Profitability is not inherently tied to billing method – it depends on efficiency and cost control. A firm that understands its workflows, delegates tasks effectively, and leverages technology can deliver fixed-fee work at a higher margin than time-based billing.

For example, a corporate transaction that would cost £300,000 in hourly time might be priced at £350,000 fixed, but completed with 20 percent fewer internal hours due to process automation. The result – a higher margin and a happier client.

Myth 2: Fixed fees are just discounts

Fixed fees do not have to mean lower prices. The goal is not to reduce cost but to provide cost clarity. A well-structured fixed fee often commands a premium because it includes risk-sharing and operational discipline. When framed correctly, clients see fixed fees as value-added, not price cuts.

Myth 3: Fixed fees only work for simple work

This misconception stems from poor scoping practices. Even complex matters can be priced predictably if broken into phases or deliverable-based stages. For example:

- In litigation, fees can be fixed per stage – pleadings, discovery, pre-trial motions, and trial.

- In M&A, due diligence, drafting, and regulatory approvals can each have a separate fixed price.

Myth 4: Clients distrust fixed fees
Some firms fear that clients will assume fixed fees are inflated "safety nets". In practice, clients appreciate transparency. Explaining how a fee was calculated, what assumptions were made, and how variations will be managed builds trust rather than suspicion.

Myth 5: Fixed fees limit flexibility
On the contrary, fixed fees encourage creative pricing design. Hybrid models (fixed for predictable phases and capped hourly for uncertain elements) can balance both firm and client interests. Flexibility lies in structuring the arrangement, not in clinging to hourly billing.

Myth 6: Fixed fees mean "all-in" work
There is a mistaken belief that a fixed fee obliges the lawyer to handle anything and everything that arises for that price. This is incorrect. Fixed fees are always subject to a carefully defined scope, and any work outside of that scope must be discussed and priced separately.

The economics of fixed fees
The success of fixed fees lies not in guessing the right number but in designing a model that aligns efficiency, risk management, and value perception. For many firms, this requires unlearning decades of habits formed around hourly billing and embracing a more commercial approach.

Profitability drivers under fixed models
Unlike hourly billing, where revenue is a direct function of time, fixed fees reward operational control. Profitability depends on:
- *Scope clarity.* Defining exactly what is and is not included.
- *Process efficiency.* Streamlining work through smart delegation and technology.
- *Experience.* Using insights from similar past matters to price accurately and avoid underestimation.

For example, a litigation firm handling complex discovery might integrate e-discovery platforms to reduce manual review time by 50 percent. Under hourly billing, this efficiency would reduce billable hours and revenue. Under a fixed fee, however, the firm captures more margin by completing the work in less time.

Shifting the value conversation

Fixed fees encourage firms to focus less on how many hours they invest and more on the outcomes they deliver. This shift benefits both sides:

- Clients gain certainty and confidence in the value of the result.
- Firms gain freedom to innovate, automate, and optimize processes without worrying about billable time leakage.

A partner in a UK corporate firm summarized it succinctly: *"Fixed fees forced us to understand what each task really costs – and where we can be more efficient. It's changed our view of profitability for the better."*

Data as the foundation of pricing

To price effectively, firms need historical data on:

- Average time and cost for each type of matter.
- Resource allocation patterns (partner v. associate involvement).
- Common risks or variations encountered.

Unfortunately, many firms lack this baseline. Developing matter-cost databases is often the first step towards sustainable fixed pricing. Firms that ignore data risk either overpricing (losing work) or underpricing (eroding margin).

Benefits for law firms

The benefits of fixed fees extend far beyond meeting client demands. When implemented with discipline, they can enhance client loyalty, improve financial predictability, and strengthen the firm's competitive position.

Stronger client relationships

Fixed fees signal alignment with the client's priorities. They show the firm is willing to share risk rather than pushing all uncertainty onto the client. This fosters:

- *Trust.* Clients appreciate transparency and proactive communication.
- *Collaboration.* With cost concerns removed, conversations focus on strategy and outcomes.

- *Long-term loyalty.* Clients are more likely to engage firms that offer predictability in subsequent matters or panel reviews.

A study of large corporates by Acritas found that predictable pricing is one of the top three factors influencing law firm loyalty.

Revenue predictability
For firms, fixed fees provide more predictable revenue streams, which are particularly valuable for planning cashflow and resource allocation. Hourly billing can create peaks and troughs in revenue tied to unpredictable workflows. Fixed retainers or phased fees smooth out these fluctuations.

Market differentiation
In competitive tenders, pricing structure can be the deciding factor. Offering a carefully designed fixed fee demonstrates commercial sophistication. It differentiates the firm as client-focused and modern – particularly when competitors continue to offer only hourly models.

Internal efficiency and culture
Fixed fees incentivize firms to rethink workflows. This often leads to:
- Greater use of project management tools and specialist project management expertise.
- Better delegation to junior lawyers and paralegals.
- Embracing technology for tasks like document automation or due diligence.

Over time, these operational improvements not only enhance profitability under fixed pricing but also benefit the firm's broader service delivery model.

Risks and challenges for law firms
Despite the clear advantages, fixed fees also carry risks. Firms that implement them without proper planning can suffer financial or reputational damage.

The danger of underpricing
The most obvious risk is underestimating the work required. A single poorly scoped fixed fee can erode months of profit from other engagements. This often stems from:

- Overconfidence or lack of data.
- Underestimating complexity.
- Scope creep caused by ambiguous boundaries.

Scope creep and client expectations

Scope creep is one of the biggest challenges in fixed pricing. Without well-defined deliverables and variation protocols, clients may assume that additional work is included. This is particularly problematic when multiple stakeholders are involved and expectations shift mid-matter.

A mitigation strategy could involve the following:
- Document scope boundaries clearly.
- Include specific variation triggers (e.g., material changes in complexity).
- Have proactive conversations about emerging issues rather than surprising clients with extra charges at the end of the matter.

Cultural resistance

Partners often resist fixed fees because they are accustomed to tracking and monetizing time. Shifting to a model where efficiency, not hours, drives profit requires a cultural transformation. This includes:
- Training partners to scope and price accurately.
- Showing data on profitability of well-executed fixed models.
- Aligning internal incentives (e.g., rewarding margin and client satisfaction rather than billable hours alone).

Managing high-uncertainty matters

Not all matters lend themselves to fully fixed pricing. Complex, multi-year litigation, for example, involves many unpredictable factors. However, this does not mean fixed pricing is impossible. Firms can adopt hybrid models – fixed fees for early phases (e.g., pleadings, discovery) with capped or blended rates for later, more uncertain stages.

Scoping discipline and model design

Scoping is the foundation of fixed fee success. Without precise, data-informed scoping, even the best-intentioned fixed fee arrangement can unravel.

The art and science of scoping

Scoping requires both quantitative analysis (data on hours, costs, and risks) and qualitative judgment (experience, market knowledge, and client priorities). Key steps include:

1. *Break the matter into components.* Each phase or deliverable is priced separately.
2. *Identify risks and unknowns.* Build contingency buffers into the price.
3. *Engage the client in defining scope.* Collaborative scoping prevents misunderstandings.
4. *Document assumptions.* A clear record of assumptions ensures fairness if variations occur.

Pricing models to consider

- *Fixed phase pricing.* Assigning fixed fees to each stage of a project or dispute.
- *Tiered packages.* Offering basic, standard, and premium levels of service.
- *Blended retainers.* A fixed monthly fee covering defined categories of work.
- *Hybrid approaches.* Combining fixed elements with capped hourly rates or success-based fees.

Each model offers different advantages. For example, tiered packages provide clients with choice, which can psychologically enhance perceived control and satisfaction.

In an M&A transaction, a firm might structure fees as follows:

- £50,000 fixed for due diligence.
- £75,000 fixed for drafting and negotiation.
- £25,000 fixed for regulatory compliance and closing.

This modular approach reassures the client that costs are contained, while allowing the firm to manage workload efficiently.

Communicating and defending the fixed fee

Even a well-structured fixed fee can fail commercially if it is not communicated effectively. Many partners underestimate the importance of narrative and framing in pricing conversations. The way the fee is presented – its context, structure, and perceived fairness – often matters more than the number itself.

Framing the value proposition

When presenting a fixed fee, the emphasis should not be on the cost alone but on what the client receives in return. For example:

> *"This fee provides complete coverage of all key regulatory steps, with guaranteed turnaround times and 24/7 partner availability during critical closing stages. There will be no additional charges unless the scope materially changes."*

By linking the fee to tangible benefits, you shift the conversation away from a cost comparison and towards the value and security the client is buying.

Anticipating objections

Some clients, especially those new to fixed pricing, may worry that the fee contains "hidden padding" to account for unforeseen work. This can be addressed by:

- Explaining the scoping process and the assumptions made.
- Breaking the fee down into phases or components, showing how the price aligns with anticipated workload.
- Offering a variation mechanism (e.g., "If X occurs, we will revisit pricing in consultation with you").

By proactively addressing these concerns, the firm demonstrates transparency and fairness.

The psychology of choice

When appropriate, consider presenting multiple fixed fee options – for example, a basic, standard, and premium package. This approach:

- Gives clients a sense of control.
- Creates reference points that make the standard option feel balanced and reasonable.
- Encourages conversation around value rather than price haggling.

Case illustration

A mid-sized UK firm pitching for a multi-jurisdictional merger presented three fixed fee tiers:

1. *Basic (£200,000).* Core legal due diligence and documentation.
2. *Standard (£250,000).* Basic services plus regulatory liaison and post-merger integration advice.

3. *Premium (£300,000)*. All services plus dedicated project management and weekly executive briefings.

Over 80 percent of clients opted for the standard tier, boosting the firm's average margin compared to hourly billing while satisfying client demand for transparency and choice.

Technology and data analytics as enablers

Accurate fixed fee pricing is impossible without robust data and process visibility. Historically, law firms have operated with limited data on time and cost at the matter level, often relying on "gut feel" to set fees. In today's competitive environment, that approach is no longer tenable.

Historical data as a strategic asset

Data from past matters allows firms to:

- Determine average costs and timeframes for specific types of work.
- Identify inefficiencies and opportunities for automation.
- Set realistic margins while remaining competitive.

Firms that invest in building pricing databases – even starting with simple time and cost analyses – quickly gain an edge in fixed fee proposals.

Real-time tracking and monitoring

One of the biggest risks in fixed fee engagements is scope overrun. Project management tools such as Virtual Pricing Director® allow firms to:

- Track progress and costs in real time.
- Identify early warning signs of budget stress.
- Reallocate resources before issues escalate.

This proactive oversight ensures profitability and keeps clients informed.

The role of AI and predictive analytics

Artificial intelligence and machine learning have transformed legal pricing. Platforms like Virtual Pricing Director® provide:

- Automated cost modelling based on historical data.
- "What-if" scenario planning for different fee structures.
- Margin analysis and predictive insights for profitability management.

These tools not only enhance pricing accuracy but also improve credibility in client discussions by showing that the firm's fee is data-driven, not arbitrary.

Technology as a differentiator
Clients increasingly expect their advisers to leverage technology for both service delivery and pricing. A firm that can demonstrate a data-backed approach to fixed fees is seen as modern, efficient, and strategically aligned with business priorities.

Culture, mindset, and capability building
Transitioning to fixed fees requires more than new pricing models – it demands a cultural shift within the firm. For many lawyers, the billable hour has shaped not only how they charge but how they think about their own value.

Overcoming hourly billing bias
Hourly billing creates a psychological comfort zone. Lawyers see a direct connection between time spent and revenue earned. Fixed fees disrupt this dynamic, requiring lawyers to:
- Focus on efficiency rather than effort.
- Develop commercial awareness of cost drivers and margins.
- Take ownership of pricing outcomes, not just legal outcomes.

Training and development
To thrive under fixed pricing, partners and associates need:
- *Scoping skills.* Knowing how to break down a matter into clearly defined tasks and deliverables.
- *Commercial literacy.* Understanding how fees, costs, and margins interact.
- *Behavioral pricing expertise.* Learning how to frame, present, and negotiate fixed fees persuasively.

Workshops, simulations, and pricing academies can accelerate this learning. Role-playing client conversations is particularly effective for building confidence.

Aligning incentives

Firms must review how they reward lawyers. If compensation is based solely on billable hours, fixed pricing will always be viewed as a threat rather than an opportunity. Alternative metrics might include:
- Client satisfaction scores.
- Profitability of matters.
- Efficiency gains and collaboration.

Cultural benefits of fixed fees

Firms that embrace fixed pricing often report better collaboration between teams. When revenue is not tied to individual hours, lawyers are incentivized to share knowledge, use automation tools, and delegate effectively. Over time, this cultural shift leads to higher quality outcomes and stronger client relationships.

Case studies, competitive advantage, and future outlook

Case Study 1: Litigation firm boosting margins with fixed phases

A mid-tier litigation firm segmented its standard litigation workflow into five phases, each with a fixed fee. Over 18 months:
- Client complaints about cost overruns dropped by 70 percent.
- Realization rates improved by 15 percent as scope creep was better controlled.
- The firm saw increased referrals from satisfied in-house counsel.

Case Study 2: Corporate firm winning panels through predictability

A global corporate firm secured a coveted panel position with a financial services giant by offering fixed annual retainers for advisory work. The client praised the firm's "businesslike approach to budgeting", which allowed them to integrate external legal spend into financial forecasts seamlessly.

Case Study 3: Hybrid models for complex transactions

A boutique M&A firm used a hybrid structure – fixed pricing for due diligence and negotiation, combined with success-based fees for deal completion. This structure aligned the firm's incentives with the client's business goals and created a win-win pricing environment.

Competitive advantage of predictability

Predictable pricing is increasingly a must-have for winning tenders and RFPs. In many competitive reviews, procurement teams heavily weight pricing structure and transparency, sometimes even more than headline costs. Firms that can present a compelling fixed fee proposal often gain a decisive edge.

Predictability also builds brand differentiation. Clients see firms offering fixed fees as progressive, client-centric, and aligned with modern business practices.

The future of fixed fees

Looking ahead, fixed fees will evolve in three key ways:

1. *Integration with value-based pricing.* Fixed fees will increasingly be tied to outcomes, KPIs, or business impact, moving beyond task-based pricing.
2. *Technology-driven precision.* AI tools will make cost modelling more accurate, enabling firms to price even complex matters with confidence.
3. *Client collaboration.* We will see more co-designed pricing models where firms and clients jointly agree on scope, milestones, and value metrics.

The firms that succeed will be those that treat fixed pricing not as a concession but as a strategic discipline, investing in data, capability, and cultural change.

Why technology solutions have emerged

The growing demand for fixed fees and pricing predictability has exposed a critical capability gap within many law firms – the ability to accurately calculate, model, and defend fixed fee proposals without jeopardizing profitability. Partners often lack:

- Reliable historical data on matter costs.
- The time and tools to model multiple pricing scenarios.
- The confidence to communicate complex pricing structures to clients.

In response to this gap, platforms like Virtual Pricing Director® (VPD) have been developed to bring a new level of precision, transparency, and confidence to legal pricing.

Bridging the data gap

One of the biggest challenges in fixed fee pricing is the absence of accurate matter-level data. VPD addresses this by:

- Capturing and analyzing historical time and cost data across the firm.
- Providing benchmarks and predictive analytics for similar matters.
- Enabling partners to build data-backed fee proposals that reflect real-world complexity and resource requirements.

This means partners no longer rely on "gut feel" or conservative padding when setting fees, reducing both client suspicion and the risk of under-pricing.

Scenario modeling for profitability

VPD allows partners to create multiple pricing scenarios – fixed, phased, hybrid, or retainer – while instantly visualizing the profitability and resource implications of each model. This empowers firms to:

- Identify the most commercially advantageous structure.
- Adjust for contingencies and scope variations in real-time.
- Align pricing strategy with client expectations and internal margin goals.

This dynamic modelling capability is critical when responding to RFPs, panel pitches, or high-stakes negotiations where pricing transparency is a key decision factor.

Enhancing partner confidence and client communication

Pricing conversations can be uncomfortable for many partners, particularly when moving away from the familiar language of hourly rates. VPD provides clear, client-ready proposals that:

- Break down the structure of the fee into logical components.
- Highlight the value delivered in each phase.
- Support a narrative around certainty, efficiency, and shared risk.

By equipping partners with these tools, firms can shift the pricing dialogue from defensive explanations to confident value propositions.

Driving a firm-wide pricing transformation

Technology solutions like VPD are more than pricing calculators – they are strategic enablers of cultural change. They encourage partners to think commercially, leverage data, and approach pricing as a competitive advantage rather than an administrative chore.

In an environment where clients demand transparency and value, platforms like VPD give firms the ability to compete, win, and grow profitably while meeting modern client expectations.

Conclusion

Fixed fees and predictability have moved from the margins to the mainstream of legal pricing. They are now central to how clients evaluate, select, and retain law firms. For clients, they provide peace of mind, budgetary control, and a clearer link between cost and value. For firms, they offer opportunities for margin improvement, market differentiation, and deeper client relationships – provided they are executed with rigor and transparency.

The firms that will thrive in this environment are those that:

- Invest in scoping and data analytics to ensure accuracy and profitability.
- Train partners to communicate fixed fees persuasively and confidently.
- Leverage technology and project management to deliver work efficiently.
- Shift their culture from cost recovery to value creation.

In a competitive and fast-changing market, predictable pricing is not just a client demand – it is a hallmark of modern, commercially astute legal practice.

Reference

1   www.law.com/corpcounsel/2019/03/07/lexisnexis-general-counsel-talks-legal-tech-sticking-to-a-budget-and-the-rise-of-in-house-counsel/

Chapter 9:

Partner compensation and its impact on pricing strategies

By Timothy B. Corcoran, Corcoran Consulting Group

When I was a young office cubicle dweller, if my travel schedule allowed, I was an enthusiastic participant in my company's sports teams that played in our community's recreational leagues. One winter morning, after a weather-related flight cancellation, I was in the office unexpectedly. The captain of the company's basketball team stopped by to ask if I could be available to play that evening. The storm that cancelled my flight also impacted local roads, so several players were unable to make it. I didn't have any athletic wear in the office, but there was a sporting goods store nearby, so I agreed to play.

After a busy workday, I dashed to the sports store. I picked up some athletic wear and then visited the shoe department. Cheap basketball shoes lead to sore feet, but I already had a very comfortable pair at home, so I didn't want to spend too much. I asked the amiable guy working the floor to bring me several inexpensive pairs in my size and, for comparison, a pair of the new model of the pricey shoes I already owned. When it comes to athletic apparel, price is sometimes a function of brand strength, and sometimes a function of quality. In this case, none of the cheap shoes came close to the comfort of the expensive, name-brand shoes. I needed to decide quickly – buy a cheap pair that, due to inevitable blisters and sore feet, I would wear once and probably never again or buy another pair of the expensive basketball shoes that I would surely wear when my current pair eventually wore out but would also strain my limited budget.

This is what economists call a "utility maximization" calculation. I reluctantly determined that the marginal utility of the more expensive shoes was not worth the sizable price difference. So, with a heavy sigh I told the salesman I'd take one of the cheaper pairs. He paused, told me he could see I really wanted the name-brand shoes, and then, to my astonishment, offered a substantial price discount. Suddenly the calculation changed! The price differential between the undesirable cheap shoes and the name-brand nicer shoes was now well within my "justification zone", so I immediately agreed, and I was soon out the door heading to my game.

A few years later, that sporting goods store was out of business, its assets scooped up by a larger rival. I have no specific insight into the reasons why, but the local buzz at the time was that store management, in a bid to remain competitive with big box retailers, had shifted incentives for department managers and salespeople to encourage revenue over profit. As a result, for floor employees, earning a sales commission today for selling a pair of shoes at a heavily discounted price was more appealing than waiting an uncertain number of days or weeks for the buyer who'd pay the undiscounted price, even though this sale would generate a higher commission, particularly since the difference between the two commissions wasn't sizable. Evidently, local buyers quickly learned, before viral social media, that this store was the place to go for premium goods at bargain prices.

The store's sales volume spiked, but profits evaporated, and the store closed. Presumably, store management had hoped that increased foot traffic of shoppers seeking bargains for some products would translate into increased sales of other products that retained premium prices or generated higher margins. But this can't be left to random chance. Automobile dealers often offer better price discounts or rebates when buyers agree to purchase a third-party warranty or secure dealer financing – two offerings that offer substantially higher profits to dealers than automobile sales. The buyer doesn't get the discount without the bundled purchase. By contrast, the discount for my pricey basketball shoes was offered with no strings attached. I was under no obligation to purchase an expensive NBA-official basketball, a Michael Jordan jersey, or any "If the shoe falls apart within six months, we'll replace it at half price" warranty. Bargain hunters, by definition, don't turn into premium buyers even when they really like their bargain purchases.

Incidentally, our team captain successfully recruited several other backup players who were more skilled than I, so I barely made it off the bench. In the final analysis, I could have worn my black lace-up dress shoes to play basketball that day, and my contribution would have been no different.

Unlike the sporting goods store, most law firms aren't teetering on the brink of insolvency due to terrible pricing decisions and a focus on revenue while ignoring profits. Still, law firm leaders and partners make plenty of poor pricing decisions, often because they incentivize the generation of revenue while not fully understanding the downstream impact of these incentives on firm profits. To better understand the causal relationships between pricing legal services and partner incentives, we first need to explore why law firms operate the way they do.

Following the R.U.L.E.S.

The variability in how law firm partner compensation or remuneration plans are designed and administered is wide, but the number of performance metrics in play is surprisingly narrow. In my work analyzing and recalibrating law firm incentive plans, I've consistently observed billable hour revenue and origination credit to be the two leading drivers of partner compensation, with everything else lumped together in a category that's often inaccurately characterized as "intangible" contributions.

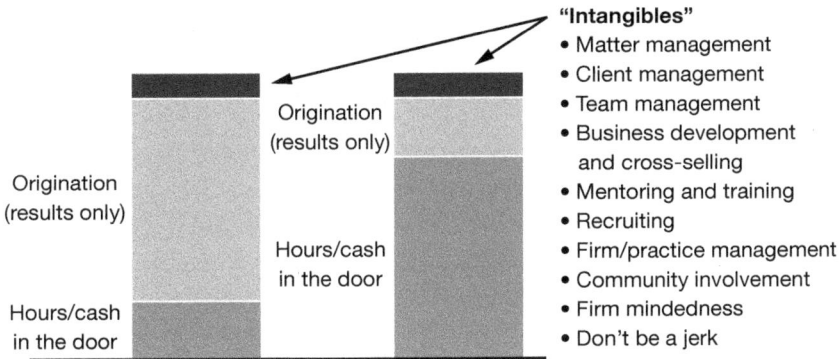

Figure 1. Common performance metrics of partner compensation plans. Source: Corcoran Consulting Group LLC.

On the one hand, this is not surprising. The traditional economic model of law firms is almost entirely reliant on lawyers generating billable hour revenue from new clients or generating billable hour revenue from new matters for existing clients. In both circumstances, it's necessary for lawyers to sell the firm's legal work and it's also necessary for lawyers to perform the legal work. To state the obvious – lawyers skilled at selling legal work can't be successful without capable lawyers doing the work and lawyers skilled at doing the work can't be successful without capable lawyers finding new engagements.

On the other hand, law firms are not simple businesses to run. There has always been a need for capable lawyers to manage and mentor the firm's lawyers and staff, to tend to the firm's financial affairs and daily operations, to select and oversee the firm's information and technical resources, and to maintain the firm's visibility through community involvement. These are not inconsequential contributions. In today's hyper-competitive market, doing these things well is harder than ever. Why, then, do lawyers so often overlook these contributions when allocating rewards?

In most law firms, the choice to emphasize production and origination over all else is not the result of an extended debate among the partners, informed by a detailed calculation of the relative economic value of various contributions. Rather, inertia and a desire to avoid the risk of a messy rewrite of partner incentives leads most firms to make minor tweaks rather than fundamentally alter a hierarchy that's been in place for years. In law firms where there has been such a discussion, the determination to stay the course or restrict changes to minor tweaks only is almost always a result of under-informed analysis competing with passionate advocacy by those treated well by the current system. It's not a fair fight. Lawyers are smart people, often employing smart people with excellent financial acumen, so why would they rely on an under-informed analysis to guide their decisions? They're starting with the wrong premise and debating the wrong issues.

The traditional economic model of law firms is captured in the acronym R.U.L.E.S., which stands for Utilization, Realization, Leverage, Expenses, and Speed of collections, though the first two factors have been reversed to make the acronym more memorable. These five factors comprise the fundamental building blocks of law firm finance. The model begins with an assessment of the firm's revenue potential, which is sizable, and then incorporates each of the above factors as a deduction against this potential revenue, until what's left is the profit pool available to the partners to share. This transition from a large amount of potential revenue to a smaller amount of distributable profit is often depicted as a "waterfall", as seen in Figure 2.

The firm's total revenue potential is calculated with a simple formula:

Rates × Hours × Timekeepers

Multiplying the billing rate for each of the firm's timekeepers by the target number of billable hours that each timekeeper is expected to generate produces the maximum revenue for the firm that year, absent a change to one of the three factors in the formula. Of course, this maximum revenue amount is only possible if every timekeeper works, bills, and collects at the target amount. This never happens.

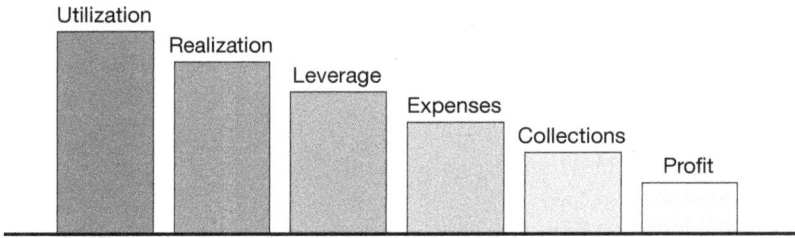

Figure 2. The R.U.L.E.S. economic model of law firms.
Source: Corcoran Consulting Group LLC.

Utilization is the measurement of how much each timekeeper works relative to the target amount. If a timekeeper is expected to work 2,200 hours but works only 1,950 hours, that timekeeper has an 89 percent utilization rate. In many law firms, individuals and practices are measured on their utilization, or "busyness" as some call it. It's obviously better for timekeepers to be working rather than idle, but as a practical matter, utilization rates are often an illusion. If an individual, a practice, or a firm truly operated at maximum utilization, there would literally be no availability to take on a single new matter. When lawyers take on new matters despite high utilization, it's not magic. Either some timekeepers work more than their target amount, or some timekeepers stop doing what they were doing to focus on the new matter. It's often both. According to Clio, a service provider focused primarily on small firms, the average US law firm utilization rate in 2024 was 37 percent.[1]

Realization is the measurement of how much of each timekeeper's work is billed and collected. If a timekeeper works 1,950 hours and bills 1,600 hours, the timekeeper has a billing realization rate of 82 percent. If the timekeeper then invoices clients for all 1,600 billable hours and collects revenue equivalent to 1,350 hours at the standard billing rate, the timekeeper has a collection realization rate of 84 percent. According to Clio, the average billing realization for US law firms in 2024 was 88 percent, and the average collection realization rate was 91 percent. According to an American Bar Association article that summarized several sources, in 2023 AmLaw 100 law firms experienced the biggest decrease in realization rates in five years.[2]

Leverage is the ratio of law firm partners to non-partner timekeepers who are billing time to client matters. Law firms with higher leverage, meaning fewer partners and more non-partners, generate more profits. While partners tend to enjoy higher billing rates than non-equity partners and associates, partners are also more costly. A partner who delegates work to several junior lawyers, each with lower billing rates and lower compensation than the partner, may generate more top-line revenue for the firm, may generate more bottom-line profit to be shared with all partners, or may generate both. So why is leverage considered reductive rather than additive to a law firm profit pool? According to one accounting expert well-versed in law firm finance, "Leverage is the greatest under-utilized tool in growing a profitable, sustainable law firm".[3] One of the most insidious conflicts inherent in the traditional financial model is that partner compensation plans routinely offer higher rewards to partners who boost their individual productivity while the firm enjoys greater profits for all partners when partners delegate more work.

Expenses, or overhead, refer to the operating costs of the law firm. It's no surprise that tightly managing a law firm's expenses leaves more distributable profit for the partners to share. Proportionally, however, the amount of profits lost from poorly managed utilization, poorly managed realization, and poor leverage dwarfs the amount of profits that can be recaptured by eliminating free coffee for the staff or reducing headcount to mirror the lawyer-to-staff ratio at a dissimilar firm with dissimilar practices serving dissimilar clients. Yet, attacking overhead to boost profits is a very popular idea among partners, because it shifts focus away from the poor management of their own practices.

Collections, characterized as the Speed of collections to complete the acronym, refers to the aging of law firm receivables. Partners all over the world are notably reluctant to pursue clients to collect unpaid invoices. Some partners fear this will provoke a discussion about the firm's billing rates and the business value delivered for these rates and lead to write-offs. Other partners find the whole topic of collections and the profitability of legal services to be unseemly, preferring to focus on their professional responsibilities that, if performed well, will overcome any client objections and deliver a handsome income... or so they were told by one of their mentors a generation ago. As a consequence, around 40 percent of some law firms' annual receivables aren't collected until the last six weeks of the fiscal year. Like any business, the longer a law firm waits to collect its fees, the higher the likelihood of write-offs. Partners whose compensation plan focuses on "cash in the door" have a huge incentive, and often free reign, to heavily discount outstanding invoices in return for prompt payment before the close of the firm's fiscal year.

The R.U.L.E.S., or waterfall, approach to law firm finance explicitly focuses on production inputs. The most common performance metrics used to evaluate partner performance refer to hours worked, how much was billed, how much was billed at the standard rate, and how much was collected. Many partner compensation plans lack any measurement of matter profitability, which would benefit from leverage. Many also lack any sophisticated measurement of fiscal hygiene, meaning the revenue figure used to assess partner performance is the amount of fees collected, not the amount of fees that could have or should have been collected. Two partners who collected USD $1 million are often deemed equivalent, even if one partner earned a 45 percent profit margin and a 97 percent overall realization rate for 1,800 hours of billed time while keeping three associates busy, while the other generated a 22 percent profit margin and a 68 percent overall realization rate for 1,400 hours of billed time with no delegation, causing three associates to fall short of their own billable hour targets.

This approach to monetizing legal experience imposes significant limits on a law firm's ability to adapt to changing times. If partners are incentivized to engage in behaviors that reduce rather than grow the amount of distributable profits, there's even more pressure to fill the waterfall by generating ever-increasing amounts of top-line revenue. Firms can grow top-line revenue by increasing hourly billing rates, by increasing the target hours each timekeeper must bill and collect, and by increasing the number of working timekeepers. Most firms are unable to raise rates across the board every year without suffering client backlash and attrition. Most firms can't demand that their lawyers bill 3,000 hours each year. However, firms have complete control over the number of timekeepers they employ. Not surprisingly, this "strategy" has led to an unprecedented number of law firm mergers and a highly lucrative market for laterals willing to change firms. However, when the three primary levers for growth are rates, hours, and timekeepers, and the firm has limited flexibility with rates and hours, adding timekeepers isn't a strategy at all... it's all that's left!

The price of misguided metrics

The inadequacy of partner compensation plans to drive profitable, sustainable business performance doesn't stop there. Poorly aligned incentives don't merely fail to reward contributions that grow profits – they often explicitly promote contributions that specifically decrease profits. Several are integrally related to the pricing of legal matters.

A common manifestation of the inherent risk aversion of law firm partners everywhere is that they closely monitor and mirror the actions of their peers and competitors. As any service provider to law firms knows, it's nearly impossible to interest partners in a new idea, no matter how innovative it may be, or how much it'll boost the firm's financial performance, unless the partners can confirm that other law firms they respect have successfully tried it first. As I have written previously, law firms are often in a race to be first to be second![4] With that in mind, it's perplexing that law firm managers tend to ignore what other law firms are doing and instead focus solely inward when it comes to evaluating a key partner contribution. This is depicted in Figure 3.

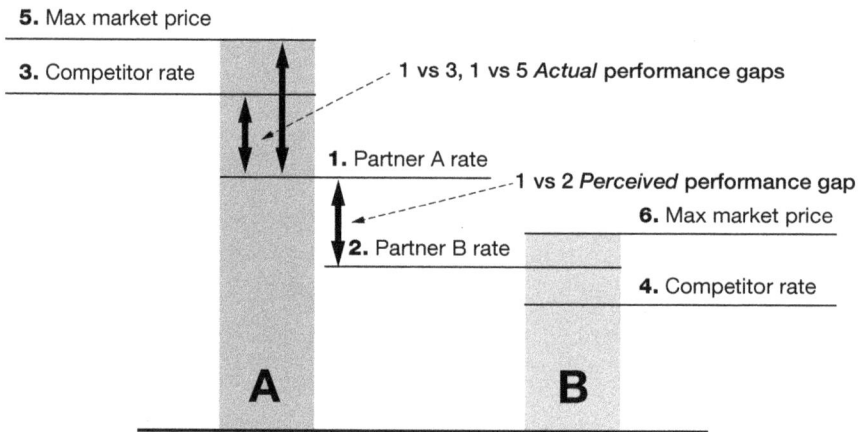

5. Max market price

3. Competitor rate   1 vs 3, 1 vs 5 *Actual* performance gaps

1. Partner A rate

1 vs 2 *Perceived* performance gap

6. Max market price

2. Partner B rate

4. Competitor rate

A   **B**

Figure 3. Misguided incentives can lead to misguided billing rates.
Source: Corcoran Consulting Group LLC.

As noted previously, partner compensation plans that place undue focus on what was collected rather than what should have been collected tend to foster poor behaviors. Relatedly, a common source of tension in many law firms is the disparity in billing rates among different practices and offices. Figure 3 illustrates a common misperception about partner performance related to billing rates. The left column shows Partner A's standard billing rate (point 1) to be much higher than Partner B's standard billing rate shown in the right column (point 2). In many firms, the analysis stops here. Partners with high billing rates regularly lament how much income they lose by "subsidizing" lower-rate partners. Since the amount of compensation earned by the higher-rate partner is not higher than the lower-rate partner by the same proportion as the difference in their respective billing rates, it must mean that the higher-rate partner is underpaid because the lower-rate partner is overpaid. It's not that simple.

A law firm is by design a multi-line business. Any business offering a wide array of products and services that offer significant differential value to buyers will have a wide range of prices. Consider Tesco in the UK or Kroger in the US, each of which offers commodities such as butter, milk, sugar, wine, rice, and other staples, while simultaneously offering premium goods in categories such as cheese, organic produce, tea, pasta, meat, seafood, ready meals, and more. It would be folly to expect a multi-product chain to affix the same price to all goods. Law firms are no different. Specifically, as a hedge against the cyclicality of business cycles, law firms embrace a range of services to increase the likelihood that revenue and profits will remain consistent, even when one or more practices or offices is experiencing a downturn. The better comparison to understand relative partner performance isn't whether Partner A or Partner B has a higher rate – it's whether each partner's rate is maximizing the market opportunity.

Partner A's billing rate is far lower than both the firm's competition (point 3) and the billing rate the client is accustomed to paying its premium law firms with the strongest brand strength (point 5). By contrast, Partner B's billing rate is higher than the firm's competition (point 4) and slightly lower than the client's stated maximum (point 6). In this context, Partner B is doing far better at securing the most favorable client rate available while Partner A is complacent, selling services at a far lower price than the market will bear. To compound the situation, Partner A may point to 100 percent realization rates ("No client has ever discounted my rate!") and to industry accolades as an endorsement of the quality of legal work offered to justify leading compensation. Ironically, to a pricing expert, 100 percent realization is as likely to indicate below-market pricing as it is to indicate above-market quality. And while the industry accolades may not permit Partner A, who works in a mid-size law firm, to match the billing rates of competitors in global behemoth law firms offering the same services, these credentials should nonetheless justify Partner A increasing the standard billing rate to reduce the gap.

There is a lot that can be done to boost the profitability of low-rate practices, but that's a topic for another chapter. For our instant purposes, the takeaway for law firm leaders is that relying primarily on internal rate comparisons as the basis for evaluating partner performance is insufficient and will drive the wrong behaviors. Partner B may feel forced to raise rates, creating a competitive disadvantage and possibly increasing write-downs and write-offs as the client corrects the firm's poor pricing decision before shifting work away from the firm. Partner A may never feel any urgency to raise rates, thereby depriving the other partners of a significant pool of distributable profit.

Market competition and client demands have motivated many law firms to explore new approaches to both the practice and business of law. As law firms test new ideas, an outdated approach to matter pricing risks eliminating much of the financial benefit. This is illustrated in Figure 4.

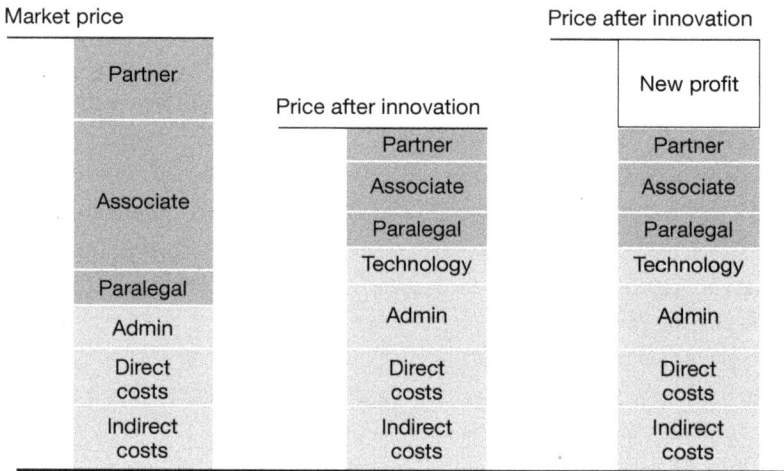

Figure 4. Misguided pricing dilutes the benefits of innovation.
Source: Corcoran Consulting Group LLC.

A few years ago, a colleague and I worked with a client to reengineer a critical but inefficient business process. This process was causing internal consternation as the firm's clients placed increasing demands for faster delivery time for a specific legal service even as they assigned an increasing volume of this work to the firm. The firm already offered a very favorable rate for the specific service, so offering a discount to appease the client was not necessary. Upon analysis, the process involved an unnecessarily high proportion of associate hours, since it was mostly an administrative task that could be performed well by non-billable administrative staff with some updated technology. It was also evident that almost no partner hours were needed, but this hadn't stopped multiple partners from billing time to this fast-growing service. This "before" state is reflected in the left column of Figure 4.

With our assistance, the process was streamlined. The firm was able to perform the service in a fraction of the previous time, at once satisfying the client's demands and freeing up capacity to take on even more of this work. It's a beautiful story that ended well for everyone. Except that's not what happened. When we returned some months later to assess progress, we learned of the increased volume of work, the client's delight with the speed of delivery, and even how the practice group had attracted several new clients because of this innovation. We also learned that the partners were, to put it kindly, annoyed with us for hurting their revenue. A key component of our innovation training was how to use innovation to simultaneously boost profits and client satisfaction, so we were baffled.

We quickly learned that the partners ignored or misunderstood the training, so when their billable hours and the associates' billable hours were eliminated from the process, they billed only for the paralegal time that remained. This is reflected in the middle column in Figure 4. The client had not asked for a discount. The service didn't have wide variability in scope, so it was a perfect candidate for a flat fee. What should have happened is reflected in the right column in Figure 4. Had the firm affixed a flat fee to the service offering, the client would not have experienced any change in price. The client may not have noticed any difference at all, since the process already had limited pricing variability. The firm's cost to deliver the same service dropped, the price should have remained intact, and the resulting profits should have dropped to the bottom line, increasing the distributable profit for all partners. The partners still weren't convinced, making vague references to ethical billing practices. We certainly weren't advocating anything unethical. The client was delighted with the price and didn't care "how the sausage was made". All they wanted was faster turnaround. In fact, increasing the speed might have justified a price increase, especially since the firm's rates were already favorable.

We consulted the firm's executive committee that assigned this innovation project to us in the first place. They had been clear that they were prepared to embrace innovation in process as well as in pricing. They then shared where the breakdown occurred. During the time elapsed from our innovation process to the point of our status update, the fiscal year ended, and a new fiscal year began. During the compensation review process, the firm's compensation committee, a distinct entity from the firm's executive committee, had specifically inquired about declining partner billings despite a fast-growing service, and subsequently imposed a compensation penalty on each of the partners involved.

When a partner compensation plan, or a compensation committee administering a compensation plan, doesn't consider the benefits of strategic pricing decisions that boost the firm's profits, the partners quickly revert to outdated models and potentially create or exacerbate competitive disadvantages relative to competitors willing to meet client expectations by embracing innovation.

Cost plus is a minus

Our final point is related to the underlying "costs plus" methodology used in many law firms to establish partner billing rates. The basis of this methodology is that the sum of the firm's operating costs added to the partners' desired profits dictate what prices to charge. When staff headcount and salaries rise, or one of the firm's offices moves to a new location with a higher lease obligation, or the firm must pay a settlement to avoid further action for the unsavory behavior of a now-departed partner, or when firm management blindly increases associate salaries to "keep pace" despite not competing for the same talent pool, the amount of profit available to distribute to partners will decrease unless the firm can generate new revenue. Yes, adding new timekeepers will generate more revenue too, but this also increases the costs. Therefore, the only possible solution is that billing rates must be increased.

In many cases, the amount of incremental revenue needed to cover the firm's increased costs is divided in a pro rata manner across all timekeepers. As noted above, given the wide range and practices and matter types, and the wide variability in clients, it would be statistically improbable, bordering on impossible, for all of a law firm's offerings to have the same perceived value in the market and therefore warrant a simultaneous and matching percentage rate increase. In fact, in the face of unprecedented competition to win and retain clients, if this is still the level of scrutiny that firm management places on something so important as developing a pricing methodology, the firm might be better served dismissing all firm managers and assigning the same task to an intern using Excel.

This lack of sophistication can be observed elsewhere, such as billing rates based on tenure. A general counsel client at a large corporation once told me, "I'll gladly pay more for better value and deeper experience. I'm not paying more simply because more time has passed since someone graduated law school." Businesses that compete ferociously for precious market share and with thin profit margins spend a great deal of time studying the market's propensity to buy at different price points. Undoubtedly there's a correlation between a lawyer's age and experience and the amount of value they bring to an engagement. However, that's not enough. Other factors matter too. For example, if a client hires five law firms to do similar work in different regions, there may be rate differences based on geographic norms. But clients quicky notice when one law firm bills partner rates for the same work that another law firm delegates to associates without any difference in quality.

When a partner compensation plan offers greater rewards to partners who hoard work that could be leveraged, this creates financial risk for both the short- and long-term. There's an immediate reduction in distributable profits for other partners because hoarding work benefits the individual partner more than it benefits the firm. Long-term, it's unlikely that the partner will be able to justify the higher rate if there's no discernable difference in quality, so the client may stop hiring the firm. If the partner retains the client by billing his or her own time at a lower associate billing rate, this often creates downward price pressure on cross-selling opportunities, since the client may expect other partners to reduce their fees accordingly.

Options for realigning incentives

A 2010 study on lawyer personality traits found that, compared to business executives, the typical lawyer looks like an individual contributor, not a manager.[5] If this isn't already evident, our review of the nature of traditional partner compensation should reveal that focusing nearly all rewards on individual contributions that may not benefit the firm, and may actively harm the firm, is not the best way to foster a firm-first ownership mentality.

An excellent starting point for law firm partners and leaders reconsidering the nature of partner incentives is to first decide whether the role of a partner is to operate as a highly paid individual contributor or as a business owner. A well-paid employee may have no obligation to ensure that other employees are busy and productive. An owner should always be mindful of the entire organization's productivity. A lawyer who is uniquely capable of doing excellent legal work may warrant high compensation. Is there any reason other than tradition that all highly compensated lawyers must also be owners? Conversely, should a lawyer with excellent business acumen, capable of managing people and resources to maximum effectiveness despite not generating significant fees individually, be prohibited from becoming an owner?

Most law firms have from time to time promoted lawyers with great promise into partner roles, only to discover that some simply do not grow into effective owners. This is not necessarily a failing. In much the same way that some lawyers self-select into one practice because they lack the skills or training to engage in another, not all lawyers are capable of being effective owners. It's incumbent on partners to assess their shared cultural values and determine what contributions are necessary to become, and remain, an owner of the law firm. From here, it's necessary to identify and reduce partner incentives that foster self-serving behavior and increase rewards for contributions that provide the greatest long-term economic value to the firm. There are many ways to define what constitutes long-term economic value, but here are some helpful guidelines. It should come as no surprise that nearly all of these guidelines can be met, at least in part, by taking a more strategic view of pricing legal services.

- Which contributions will generate long-term client loyalty and create opportunities for cross-selling?
- Which contributions will improve client satisfaction and lead to unsolicited client referrals?
- Which contributions will help unlock the economic value of the firm's junior lawyers and staff?
- Which contributions will provide the firm with a competitive advantage for its legal work? For its service posture? For its innovation?
- Which contributions will position the firm well to compete in an increasingly complex and competitive market?
- Which contributions within the organization and to the local community best embody the spirit that the partners wish to be recognizable as the firm's brand?

These questions might appear to some action-oriented lawyers to be too esoteric to have immediate practical value. But each was very likely asked and answered, in one form or another, by the founders of every successful law firm, both large and small, as they considered what kind of business they would like to run, which contributions would be critical to their success, and which values they would be prepared to hold themselves and their fellow owners accountable to uphold to ensure their new venture would not fail. It is no less important to ask these questions periodically within an established law firm to ensure that each lawyer who is or may become a fellow owner is held to the same standard of care.

Adjusting a partner compensation plan is not for the faint of heart. Even when the need to change is both critical and widely recognized by the partners, inertia is a powerful force to overcome. Despite good intentions, it's also hard for partners – as it is for anyone – to set aside their own self-interests and instinct for self-preservation and think solely of what's in the firm's best interests. No one should be surprised that the highest paid partners are concerned about protecting their current pay level. No one should be surprised when partners at or near the bottom rung of partner performance, however this is currently defined, are concerned that any change might result in their removal from the partnership. No one should be surprised that weak managers, elected more for their ability to not ruffle feathers than for their ability to boldly lead, may hesitate to challenge the status quo. It may be daunting, but an unprecedented number of law firms have recently started to reexamine partner incentives. They have realized that trying to improve innovation, client focus, and collaboration will be a fruitless exercise when partners earn higher rewards for adhering to an outdated business model.

References

1   Clio "Legal Trends" report, 2024. www.clio.com/resources/legal-trends/benchmarks/
2   Wittenberg, Dan, "The Impact of Falling Law Firm Realization Rates," August 2024. www.americanbar.org/groups/litigation/resources/litigation-news/2024/summer/impact-falling-law-firm-realization-rates/
3   Scott, John, "Law Firm Leverage: How to Overcome Common Obstacles to this Essential Profit Strategy," January 2025. https://anderscpa.com/learn/blog/law-firm-leverage/
4   Corcoran, Timothy B., "The Race to Second Place," August 2012. www.bringintim.com/corcorans-business-of-law/2012/08/the-race-to-second-place
5   Foster, Jeff; Richard, Larry; Rohrer, Lisa; Sirkin, Mark, "Understanding Lawyers: Why We Do the Things We Do," 2010. www.hoganassessments.com/sites/default/files/Lawyer_Personality_12.1_0.pdf

Chapter 10:
Aligning compensation with value

By Benjamin Viney, practice lead GB and Ireland – Work, Rewards, and Careers, WTW

"It's not about the money. We're all paid stupid amounts in the real world. This is all about how valued people feel."
Senior leader in a global law firm

The psychology of pay and value

My wife Anna spent four years writing a musical about the intrinsic value that everyone has and the way in which society ascribes value to people differently depending on where they are from, what they do in life, what they achieve, as well as a host of other factors. The musical emphasizes the fact that in so many walks of life, perceived intrinsic value is often bound up with the need to remain productive, and that, as the saying goes, "You are only as good as your last performance". Nowhere is this seen more acutely than in the realm of elite sport, where the fall from the highest peaks can be manifestly (and publicly) brutal, where the sweet taste of victory is often fleeting, and where even the most successful still need to feel valued. Sarina Wiegman, the coach of the England women's football team, which retained its European Championship crown in July 2025, delivered a speech at a reception in 10 Downing Street, expressing gratitude at the reaction the team was receiving: *"I feel so much respect from England and from the Royal family, too"*, she said later. *"I think that's the most important thing – feeling valued..."*

The psychology of value – and of feeling valued – runs deep in the human psyche. I observe this all the time in my work advising firms on compensation and performance management, where firms make assessments – usually annual – of the value of partners and associates in order to determine performance and compensation outcomes. Many partners and associates shrink from this constant cycle of evaluation, compensation, and career decisions. One of my former bosses once described the annual appraisal as

"Feedback from those who don't want to give it to those who don't want to receive it" – a mini Judgment Day, over and over again.

Another psychological aspect that has a profound impact on how people receive these decisions is equity theory, where people compare their own inputs and outcomes with those of their peers before reaching a determination as to whether the outcomes are fair. In this way, relative outcomes are held to be significantly more important than absolute ones, regardless of the amounts involved. I have found this to be true even when working with the highest paid partners – earning millions each year – in the most successful firms.

Furthermore, people discount for uncertainty, and hate losing more than they love winning. The way in which I see this manifested most frequently is in the comment, "I can't pay them less than I did last year, even if their performance is demonstrably worse".

Increasing levels of transparency

It is clear to anyone involved in making decisions about partner and associate pay and performance that they can be extremely sensitive and emotive topics. It is also clear that it is becoming more difficult to meet people's expectations as to what they think they should be paid, based on their market value. This is, in part, due to increased levels of transparency, which is driven partly by changing social norms, partly by the increase in publicly-available pay information, and partly by legislation in many countries.

One example of such legislation is the EU Pay Transparency Directive, which will affect any worker in the EU with an employment relationship, i.e. associates, business services employees, and salaried partners. The Directive – transposed by Member States into local legislation by June 2026 – includes provisions that require any EU employer to provide candidates with pay rate or range information in the job advert or prior to interview, as well as an annual requirement for the employer to inform their EU employees that they have the right to request average pay levels for colleagues undertaking work of similar or equal value, with those averages being shown separately for men and women. In addition to providing this information, EU employers must also proactively provide all employees and their representatives with percentage pay gap information covering all categories of workers in their employing entity. Where pay reporting by category of worker reveals a gender pay gap of at least five percent, and when the employer cannot justify the gap with reference to objective, gender-neutral factors – including skills, effort, responsibility, working conditions, and any other factors specific to a job – employers will have to carry out a pay assessment in cooperation with employee representatives, with any unjustified gaps remedied. The Directive requires Member States to introduce specific sanctions, including minimum fines, for non-compliance.

Under the Directive, employers should have pay structures in place to ensure that women and men are paid equally for the same work or work of equal value. This includes having robust job architecture, job levelling, pay ranges, and effective governance. Although equity partners do not fall within the scope of the Directive (where they do not have an employment relationship with their firm), I am seeing more and more firms developing structures and systems that enable them to convey to partners the things that the firm values and will be rewarded. In other words, firms are seeking to determine more systematically the basis on which evaluation and compensation decisions are made, and communicate those decisions to partners in such a way as to seek to manage the perception of fairness. The aim is to be able to attract and retain the talent firms need in a market where competition for clients and talent intensifies at a pace not seen before, and where partners and associates are increasingly willing to move to other firms.

Valuing and compensating the contributions of associates and partners

Associates

For many years, firms have valued associates with reference to market compensation rates, submitting data to a compensation survey provider such as WTW and receiving access to compensation data from other firms, on an aggregated basis. Associate salaries have been determined with reference to the relevant market for talent, e.g. Magic Circle, Silver Circle, or a specific peer group of competitor firms. Increasingly, firms have wrestled with the question as to whether all associates at a particular level – usually PQE – should be paid the same, or whether associates in some practice areas should be paid more (or less) than other practice areas, to reflect the differences that exist in diverse talent markets. This is partly a philosophical question regarding whether a firm desires to align compensation with market forces, or whether a firm seeks to hold to the traditional partnership, "We're all in this together" ethos. Given the afore-mentioned competitive pressures, I am finding that more and more firms are concluding that they have no choice but to align to different talent markets for selected parts of the firm.

Bonus payments to associates in the majority of firms I have worked with are still heavily predicated on utilization. Some firms focus on hours charged to a client code whilst others focus on hours actually billed and paid by clients. In practice, the outcome is usually similar, as the firms adopting the former approach tend to set bonus thresholds at higher levels – to take account of expected write-offs – than those adopting the latter approach.

Many firms seek to encourage associates to make wider contributions to the firm beyond utilization and often incorporate elements such as business development, innovation, and client satisfaction into their bonus schemes. To do this well requires effective performance management systems in which sufficient time and effort are devoted to achieving the right outcomes and communicating them effectively to associates. This is easier said than done. To the extent that firms move away from a reliance on the billable hour, it will become more important to ensure that they are making bonus decisions in a way that balances the perception of fairness and the time taken to achieve that outcome. As noted above, in the context of the EU Pay Transparency Directive, this will need to be done using objective, gender-neutral criteria.

A substantial body of research over many years indicates that incentives do not generally motivate performance and can have adverse effects on motivation. Bestselling author Daniel Pink writes that *"The three key elements in enduring motivation are autonomy, mastery, and purpose. Autonomy is having a measure of control over what we do and how we do it. Mastery is making progress and getting better at something that matters. Purpose is doing something that makes a difference in the world or a contribution to others."*[1]

When one considers that the pay mix in most law firms is heavily skewed towards salary – on average, 90 percent of total compensation is in the form of salary, and ten percent in the form of bonus – it is not surprising that I am asked from time to time whether firms should scrap their bonus scheme altogether and pay higher salaries. In my experience, this is almost always a bad idea. What tends to happen is that when salaries are increased there is a positive reaction initially from associates. Within a few months, the increases are forgotten and people's lifestyles adjust to their new salaries. At the end of the year, the comment is heard "Our competitors pay bonuses, so where is ours?". Then other firms increase their salaries and the firm that bought out bonuses finds that it is behind the market on total compensation, ending up in a worse position than had it not changed anything at all.

Partners

Valuing and compensating the contributions of partners is one of the thorniest issues of all. The number of firms that pay all partners equally, or according to a pure lockstep system, is shrinking all the time, in large part because of the aforementioned reasons, i.e. greater transparency and mobility between firms, but also because for this type of system to work in practice requires partners to be operating at a similar level of performance or for partners to be comfortable with the fact that there might be a weak correlation between performance and pay. I am aware of very few firms that meet these requirements. Once a firm decides not to share profits amongst partners in these ways it becomes important to determine the basis on which partners will be evaluated and compensated. This requires a system to be put in place, which is usually some form of meritocracy.

A small number of firms seek to offer market-leading compensation and attempt to attract and retain partners that will add the most economic value to their firm. In these firms there is usually a very pronounced relationship between individual financial performance and earnings. Top-earning partners earn low-to-mid eight-figure amounts, whilst other partners earn much less, e.g. a ratio of 1:20 or even 1:30 between the highest and lowest paid partners. It is not uncommon for these firms to adopt retention mechanisms such as claw backs, deferrals, or forgivable loans, whereby a substantial proportion of partner pay is contingent on partners remaining in the firm.

Most firms seek a more balanced approach, emphasizing holistic contribution and collaboration between partners. There often remains the possibility for so-called rainmakers to earn much more than other partners, but generally not to the same extent, e.g. 1:10 or 1:15 between the highest and lowest paid partners. But it is not uncommon to have a ratio as low as 1:3. It all depends on the philosophy of the partners and the range of contribution of partners within the firm.

How has partner compensation changed over the last 40 years?

In 2013, I undertook a 30-year comparison to David Maister's study on partner compensation in his book, *Managing the Professional Service Firm*,[2] and in 2023 followed this up with a 40-year comparison with my colleagues Kenneth Kuk and Sarah Huber, which we published in 2024,[3] a summary of which is included below. I am grateful to David Maister for his permission to reuse his study, which is all about identifying what value firms place on different types of partner contribution.

Eight partner archetypes were defined in Maister's study to examine the degree of earnings differentiation (see Table 1).

Table 1: The eight partner archetypes.

Partner archetype	Description
Average partner	The typical partner
Rising young superstar	Young and entrepreneurial; has built a loyal following of associates
Unproductive older partner	May have run out of gas; suspect personal problems at home
Individualistic solo operator	Likes handling high visibility projects and cases; may be slightly glib
Partner associate	Less effective in developing business; relies on other partners for opportunities
Executive committee member	Tries to do everything; major force in the firm
Struggling office leader	Manages branch office that has poor profitability
Major rainmaker	Passes clients and work on for others to handle

Further detail regarding the performance profile of each partner is set out in Table 2. In Maister's 1983 study, the eight partner archetypes were defined quantitatively and qualitatively based on their relative attributes to the average partner as shown in the table. All numbers shown are expressed as percentages of the average for all the firm's partners (Partner A).

Figures above 100 percent represent superior performance to the average partner. For example, Partner D worked five percent more billable hours than

Table 2: Additional information about each partner archetype.

	Partner A: Average partner	Partner B: Rising young superstar	Partner C: Unproductive older partner	Partner D: Individualistic solo operator	Partner E: Partner associate	Partner F: Executive committee member	Partner G: Struggling office leader	Partner H: Major rainmaker
Billable hours	100	141	74	105	115	92	95	35
Non-billable hours	100	152	51	92	60	243	156	150
Value of portfolio managed	100	198	33	45	55	129	90	112
Write-off performance	100	120	50	102	101	150	63	132
Billable time not yet billed	100	105	59	40	93	121	80	108
Cash collection	100	110	72	50	95	115	83	103
Business getting	100	200	25	73	15	175	74	312
Charge out rate	100	64	129	104	103	112	108	139
Quality of work	Average	Excellent	Average	Excellent	Average	Above average	Slightly above average	Average
External respect in community	Average	Excellent	Not known outside	Very visible	Not well known	Very well known	Thought to be well known	Superb
Cooperativeness with others	Average	Not good; somewhat territorial	Very cooperative	Not very cooperative	Very willing	Very well liked	Not perceived as cooperative	Not cooperative
Track record of developing associates	Average	Outstanding	Poor	Poor	Average	Outstanding	Not enough evidence	Not good
Committee work and firm management	Average	Not much	Willing but rarely chosen	None	Will serve whenever asked	Extensive	A great deal	Used to be involved but not any more

Source: Partner Earnings 2024: 40 years of change. WTW.

the firm average, but eight percent fewer non-billable hours. When it came to the amount of work performed for their clients but not billed, Partner D's performance was only 40 percent, far less than the firm average. Similarly, their performance on collections was 50 percent – Partner D took twice as long to collect as the average partner.

In his original work, Maister summed up the exercise of conducting the survey in a single word: confusion. He characterized the effort this way because the range of pay-related responses received for most partners varied so significantly from firm to firm.

Forty years later, the range of responses is even larger for five of the seven partner archetypes (see Figure 1 overleaf). This points to the importance of doing what is right for your firm, its history, culture, and circumstances, yet serves as a reminder to be mindful of practices that exist elsewhere. In part, this awareness helps attract talent from other firms and defends against partners being targeted by firms with more attractive pay propositions.

While we observed a general tendency to expect more from the average partner and differentiate less for partners in different archetypes, it is also important to note that firms do not appear to shy away from rewarding high-impact partners more so today than when the original study was conducted. Partners' non-financial contributions have become more important but, given the challenges in measuring impact and performance, firms often shy away from more radical decisions in these areas.

Valuing and compensating leadership roles

One of the most divisive issues I come across when helping firms to navigate partner pay is what value to place on leadership positions. In my experience, there are two extremes equally to be avoided. The first is ascribing undue importance to leadership roles, such that a perception prevails that the way to progress one's career as a partner and the way to earn more in the firm is by taking on a leadership role. In these situations, I am told that some partners are simply "chasing the badge" in order to increase their compensation. The other extreme is ascribing very limited value to leadership roles, with partners expected to undertake the position on top of their role as an individual contributor, but without making any allowance for the significant time and effort expended to fulfil the role. It is unsurprising that in these firms it is often difficult to find enough partners who are skilled and willing to take on the role. Some partners observe that they end up being financially worse off than they were before they took on the leadership position.

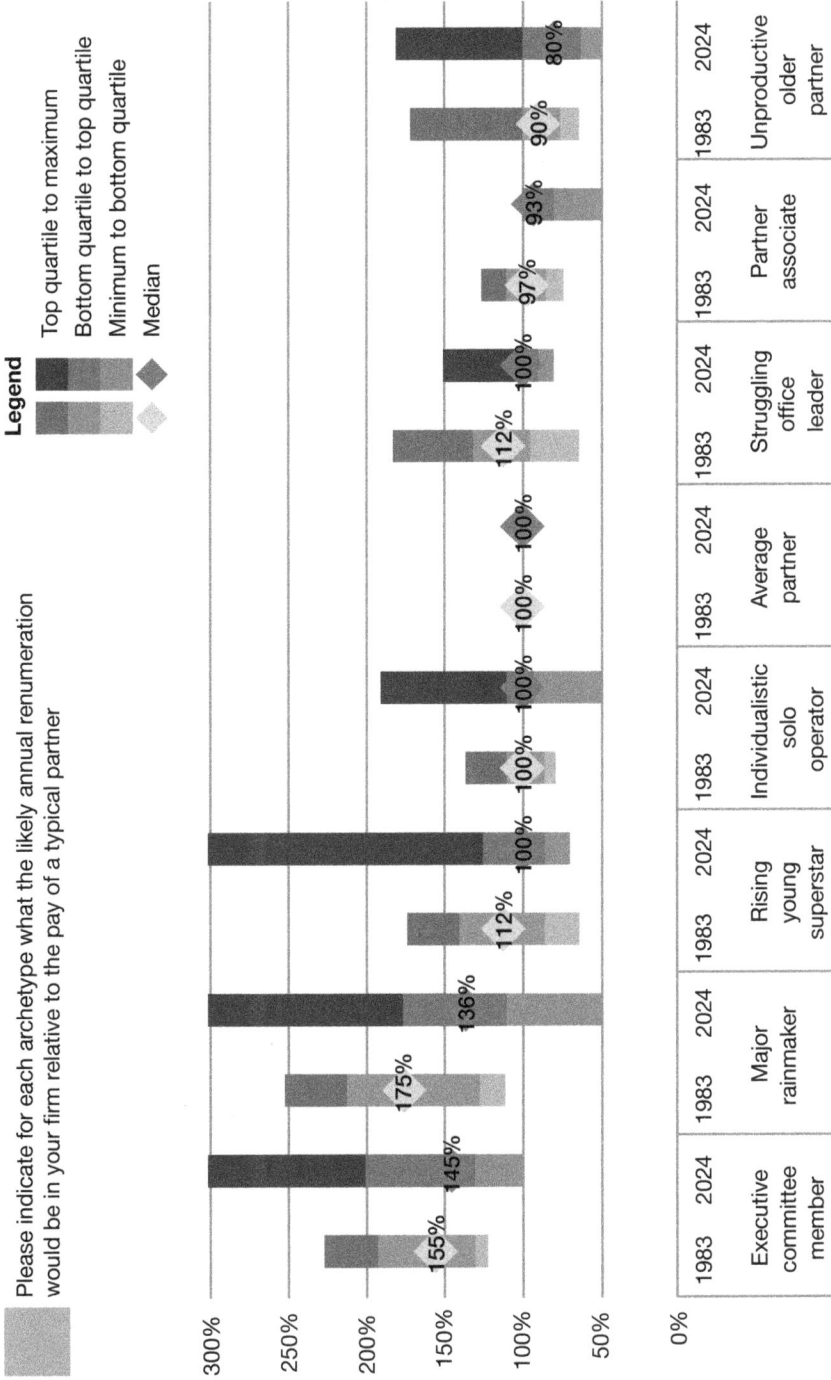

Figure 1: Range of annual earnings relative to the typical partner – 1983 vs 2024.

Please indicate for each archetype what the likely annual renumeration would be in your firm relative to the pay of a typical partner

Legend
- Top quartile to maximum
- Bottom quartile to top quartile
- Minimum to bottom quartile
- Median

Source: Partner Earnings 2024: 40 years of change. WTW.

When evaluating leadership roles, I find it helpful to keep three things in mind:

1. The fact that all partners are leaders in the firm and so a certain amount of leadership activity is expected as "part of the job". This helps to avoid situations where partners seek to claim additional credit and compensation for activities that should be taken as a given for a partner, and to ensure that the number of formal leadership roles is not excessive.

2. The size, scope, and complexity of leadership roles, which vary significantly.

3. The fact that some leadership roles tend to be helpful to a partner's individual practice whilst other leadership roles tend to be detrimental to a partner's practice. For example, a leader of an industry or sector should find that the time spent developing the firm's capabilities and brand in that sector leads to more fee-generating opportunities, including for that partner's own practice. In addition, being able to describe oneself in the market as a sector leader can be helpful in pitch meetings, business development, and other situations more generally. On the other hand, being a practice group leader or a country leader can consume a significant portion of time (if taken seriously) that often takes a partner out of the market and results in a reduction in that partner's own productivity.

A managing partner once said to me that "the best managing partners are psychologists" – they understand human behavior and how to get the best out of their people. This is especially important when considering the psychology of pay and value, as described at the beginning of this chapter. In my experience, this statement applies to any partner in a formal leadership position. If those in leadership positions can get the best of the people around them then, in my experience, this is surest way to drive sustainable revenue and profitability growth. The challenge is that the skillset required to be a successful leader is very different from the skillset required to be a successful practitioner. This raises important questions regarding the way in which firms identify, develop, select, and support those in leadership roles.

Some practical suggestions

The following practical suggestions emerge from this chapter:

1. *Determine what you will value.* A key first step is to agree what type of

firm you wish to be and the basis on which partners will share profits and reward associates. Communicate this to partners and associates and then ensure that decisions are made that are consistent with that basis.

2. *Agree minimum performance standards for partners and associates.* Unless you wish to be part of an "eat-what-you-kill" culture, this should balance financial and non-financial expectations.

3. *Identify partner personas, or archetypes.* It is important, particularly in large firms, to recognize that one-size-fits-all does not accommodate the wide range of different contributions that are of value to the firm. At the same time, I generally see firms establishing a relatively small number, e.g. three to five partner personas.

4. *Develop the right people to be leaders.* Appoint leaders who will help those around them be more successful than the sum of their parts. Consider paying leaders significantly more if they are successful than they could have earned as an individual contributor. Address any underperforming leaders even more quickly than underperforming individual contributors, as the impact on those around them is much greater.

5. *Prepare for increased transparency.* Whilst some firms are reducing transparency, it is generally much more difficult to remove transparency than to introduce it. Having said that, be cautious about increasing transparency unless you have robust systems, processes, and governance in place to manage the perception of fairness.

Above all, do not be unduly swayed by what others in the market may be doing – they will be grappling with the same challenges as you are. Seek to determine what is right for your partners and that aligns with your strategy, talent model, and culture.

References

1. Pink, Daniel. *Drive: The Surprising Truth About What Motivates Us.* Canongate Books, 2018.
2. Maister, David H., *Managing the Professional Service Firm.* Simon & Schuster, 2003.
3. Benjamin Viney, Kenneth Kuk, and Sarah Huber, "How attitudes about partner pay in professional services firms have changed", 19 June 2024. www.wtwco.com/en-gb/insights/2024/06/how-attitudes-about-partner-pay-in-professional-services-firms-have-changed

Chapter 11:
The intersection of technology and legal pricing

By Richard Burcher, founder and managing director, Validatum®, and founder and CEO, Virtual Pricing Director®

Introduction – a pricing inflection point

The legal profession is at a defining crossroads. For decades, the billable hour has served as the industry's primary pricing mechanism. It offered a simple, if blunt, instrument – multiply hours worked at an agreed rate to determine the fee. For law firms, this approach provided a predictable revenue stream and aligned with the partnership model's focus on leveraging associate time. Yet the billable hour has always been flawed. It rewards inefficiency rather than value, fails to reflect the quality of outcomes, and misaligns incentives between law firms and their clients.

The rise of advanced technologies – particularly artificial intelligence (AI) – has made these shortcomings impossible to ignore. Tasks that once took days or weeks, such as large-scale document review, contract analysis, or first-pass drafting, can now be completed in a fraction of the time. This transformation is not simply incremental – it is structural and irreversible. The efficiency and accuracy of technology are not only reducing the labor component of legal work but are also altering how clients perceive its value.

From the client's perspective, technology is both a cost saver and a leveler. Corporate legal departments, under pressure from boards and finance teams to reduce spend and provide budget certainty, now expect law firms to pass on efficiency gains. For many clients, fixed fees, capped fees, or portfolio pricing are no longer preferences but prerequisites. Procurement teams, armed with data, benchmarks, and sophisticated cost analysis, are asking hard questions: "If your AI tool completes this review in minutes, why should I pay for ten hours of associate time?".

From the law firm's perspective, this is deeply unsettling. The billable hour is more than a pricing tool – it is the foundation of how firms have historically measured productivity, distributed profits, and structured careers. A shift to fixed or value-based pricing requires new capabilities – data analytics, cost modelling, and pricing governance. It also requires a cultural change. Firms must move away from billing for time to charging for value delivered – a transition that is conceptually easy but operationally difficult.

This chapter explores these tensions in two paradigms. We first examine how technology – especially AI – is transforming legal service delivery and why this raises complex pricing challenges. It considers the hybrid human/technology model, client expectations, behavioral dynamics, and the increasing productization of legal services.

We then focus on technology as part of the solution, highlighting why traditional tools such as Excel and Excel-like legacy solutions are no longer fit for purpose and how platforms like Virtual Pricing Director® (VPD) can enable law firms to respond with sophistication, agility, and confidence.

The hybrid legal service model

Technology is reshaping the very definition of legal service delivery. Today's model is no longer defined by hours of human effort but by a blend of machine efficiency and human judgement. AI-powered tools are handling repetitive, high-volume tasks such as document classification, e-discovery, contract extraction, and compliance checks. This leaves lawyers free to focus on strategic advisory work – tasks requiring creativity, negotiation, and nuanced legal interpretation.

For clients, this hybrid model feels logical and overdue. They have embraced technology in their own organizations, from ERP systems to automated procurement platforms, and expect their law firms to do the same. They see AI as a mechanism for reducing costs and increasing predictability. A natural corollary of these expectations is the demand for fixed or capped fees. Why, they ask, should they continue to pay by the hour when technology eliminates much of that time?

From the law firm's perspective, however, this new model creates a revenue challenge. Under a time-based framework, efficiency directly erodes revenue. A due diligence exercise that once generated 200 billable hours may now require only 40. Without an alternative pricing approach, this efficiency paradox undermines profitability. Yet, paradoxically, the value of the final output – the reduced risk, the strategic insight – remains just as high, if not higher. The issue is not the intrinsic value of legal work, but how that value is measured and communicated.

A critical challenge is making the "invisible" work visible. Clients can easily measure the tangible outputs – drafts produced, meetings attended – but they cannot see the intellectual processes behind the scenes, such as the evaluation of risk scenarios, the legal creativity in structuring deals, or the oversight of AI outputs. In the hybrid era, firms must articulate the value of expertise, not just the labor required to deliver it.

The pricing conundrum of AI-enhanced services

AI-driven efficiency has decoupled price from time, forcing firms to rethink the economic logic of legal services. The billable hour model is not designed for a world where a task that previously required 20 hours of junior associate work can now be completed in 30 minutes by a machine. Clients, understandably, believe that this efficiency should be reflected in lower costs or at least in predictable, fixed pricing.

Fixed fees offer a partial solution. By disconnecting price from time, they reward efficiency and provide clients with the budget certainty they crave. But setting fixed fees correctly is difficult. It requires:

- Historical data on matter durations and costs to provide a reliable baseline.
- Scenario modelling to account for complexity and potential unknowns.
- Integration of technology costs, such as AI license fees, into the pricing structure.
- Robust scoping and change-control processes to manage variations and prevent erosion of profitability.

Many firms still guess at fixed fees or simply apply a discount to their hourly rates. This approach is unsustainable. It often leads to underpricing (which erodes profit margins) or overpricing (which alienates clients). A more sophisticated approach requires data-driven pricing systems that can model costs and risks with precision.

Another layer of complexity is client perception. Clients may assume that if AI did 80 percent of the work, the price should reflect only the remaining 20 percent. This view is misleading. The "intelligence layer" – the strategic oversight, risk evaluation, assumption of risk/liability through professional indemnity insurance, and tailored advice that lawyers provide – represents the real value. Law firms must reframe the pricing conversation, moving it away from inputs (time) to outcomes (results and risk mitigation). Done correctly, fixed fees can actually enhance profitability by aligning price with value, not effort.

Key challenges and issues in pricing hybrid legal services
Pricing hybrid services involves both operational and strategic challenges.

Transparency and trust
Clients demand clarity on how fees are calculated. Many are resistant to paying so-called "technology surcharges", arguing that AI tools, machine learning engines, and workflow automation platforms are part of the firm's infrastructure – no different from email or document management systems. From this perspective, technology is an internal enabler rather than a client-facing deliverable. Firms, therefore, face a dilemma – how to recover the considerable investment in legal tech without provoking pushback or eroding the trust that underpins the pricing discussion.

The most successful approach is often value-bundling – incorporating technology into the broader narrative of outcomes and risk mitigation, rather than listing it as a standalone line item. This reinforces the idea that the client is paying not for the tools themselves, but for the results they enable, such as faster turnaround, better quality control, reduced risk exposure, and increased cost predictability. In this model, the technology becomes part of the service's DNA – unseen but deeply valued.

However, a technology surcharge shouldn't be discounted. In some instances, it will be entirely appropriate to pass on a discrete, clearly justified technology cost – especially where the technology in question is high-value, client-specific, or materially enhances the outcome.

Precedents for this exist in other professional sectors. A patient undergoing an MRI scan in a private healthcare setting is routinely billed not just for the radiologist's time, but for use of the multimillion-pound machine itself. Similarly, when servicing a prestige vehicle, clients may incur a separate diagnostic fee tied to the use of highly specialized, capital-intensive diagnostic technology.

These analogies matter. They reinforce the idea that sophisticated tools, expertly deployed, are not incidental – they are intrinsic to the quality and reliability of the service. In legal contexts, this might include AI platforms used for high-volume due diligence, predictive litigation analytics, or compliance scanning systems tailored to the client's regulatory exposure.

Where the use of such tools demonstrably enhances accuracy, reduces risk, or materially changes the client's outcome, firms can make a credible case for transparent, technology-related charges, particularly when framed in comparison to the cost of traditional manual alternatives.

The key is transparency, framing, justification, and proportionality. If done well, this can deepen the client's appreciation of the value delivered, not diminish it.

Scope management and risk

Fixed fees transfer the risk of overruns from the client to the firm. If the scope is poorly defined or the matter becomes more complex than anticipated, the firm absorbs the cost. This makes scoping discipline, change orders, and scenario planning critical to ensuring profitability.

Commoditization

As AI tools become more widespread, clients may see legal services as interchangeable. If multiple firms can deliver the same AI-driven output, the competition may default to price. This creates a race to the bottom unless firms differentiate through expertise, client experience, and outcomes.

Internal resistance

Many law firm partners are reluctant to move away from time-based billing because it requires a shift from revenue maximization to profit management. In a partnership culture built on billable targets, this change can feel threatening. Overcoming this resistance requires both leadership commitment and tools that give partners confidence in alternative pricing models.

Behavioral and psychological dynamics

Pricing is never purely rational – it is influenced by behavioral economics and client psychology. A recurring issue is the "efficiency curse" – clients undervalue outcomes that appear easy or quick to achieve. When an AI tool completes a contract review in minutes, clients may subconsciously assume that it must be cheap, regardless of the quality or risk avoided.

Anchoring exacerbates this. Clients compare current pricing to historical bills or competitor quotes. If they paid £50,000 for due diligence last year, they resist paying the same amount this year, assuming technology has reduced the workload. Law firms must therefore re-anchor the conversation by shifting focus from "hours spent" to "value delivered". This requires storytelling around risk mitigation, quality of outcomes, and business impact.

Fixed fees can be a powerful psychological tool. By presenting a single, all-inclusive price upfront, they eliminate the negative emotions associated with time-based billing – surprise invoices, line-by-line scrutiny, and disputes over efficiency. Fixed fees also help clients perceive value by framing the service as a complete solution rather than a collection of billable increments. However, fixed fees require precision and confidence. A poorly calculated fixed fee can erode margins or damage trust if the firm tries to renegotiate mid-matter.

Emerging models and approaches

The legal market is moving towards a portfolio of pricing models, tailored to client needs and matter complexity. Among these, fixed fees have become the default request in areas such as contract management, regulatory filings, and document-heavy litigation where technology enables a degree of predictability.

Clients favor fixed fees because they align with corporate budgeting and procurement processes. For in-house legal teams under constant pressure to deliver "more for less", fixed fees reduce the administrative burden of monitoring hourly spend. Procurement professionals also prefer fixed fees because they enable direct price comparisons across firms.

However, for law firms, fixed fees require new levels of sophistication. Profitability depends on accurate forecasting of costs and risks, supported by historical data and predictive analytics. Without these tools, fixed fees become either overly cautious (and unprofitable) or too aggressive (and uncompetitive).

Beyond fixed fees, other models are gaining traction:

- *Capped fees.* A hybrid model where hourly billing applies up to a fixed limit.
- *Subscription/retainer models.* Clients pay a recurring fee for continuous access to services, often technology driven.
- *Portfolio pricing.* A single fixed fee covers multiple matters, balancing risk across a broader range of work.
- *Outcome-based or success fees.* Pricing tied to specific results, aligning incentives between firm and client.

The productization of legal services – technology as a scalable asset

One of the most profound shifts technology has enabled is the productization of legal services. Traditionally, law was a bespoke, one-off service delivered by highly trained professionals. Today, firms can package their expertise into repeatable, standardized solutions – often delivered through subscription platforms or digital tools – with little or no direct human involvement once deployed.

Examples include:

- Contract automation portals where clients input data and receive pre-vetted, firm-branded contracts.
- AI-powered compliance monitoring systems that alert clients to regulatory changes.
- Single issue legal answers – "Is this individual [insert prescribed factual matrix] an employee or an independent contractor for employment, tax, and pensions law purposes?"
- Subscription-based dashboards providing risk scores, precedent banks, or legal checklists.
- Hybrid advisory models where clients use self-service tools for routine work while reserving lawyers for high-value interventions.

From the client perspective, productization is appealing because it delivers 24/7 access, budget predictability, and cost savings. In-house teams can handle low-risk tasks internally, relying on subscription tools rather than paying for one-off advice.

For law firms, productization offers scalability and recurring revenue – a departure from the linear time-revenue model. Once a product is built, the marginal cost of serving additional clients is minimal, creating high-margin opportunities. It also strengthens client relationships, embedding the firm's expertise into the client's operations.

However, productization requires a pricing rethink. How should a firm price a subscription platform that delivers enormous value but involves little ongoing lawyer time? Traditional cost-plus pricing is irrelevant. Firms must adopt value-based pricing and may use tiered subscription models to capture different client segments.

The opportunity is significant. By combining technology, subscription access, and strategic advisory services, firms can create blended service ecosystems that lock in client loyalty and generate recurring, predictable revenue streams.

The inadequacy of traditional tools (Excel and beyond)

The majority of law firms still rely on Excel spreadsheets or basic practice management reports to handle pricing. These tools may suffice for rudimentary estimates but are wholly inadequate for the dynamic, client-centric, and profit-focused pricing landscape that hybrid legal services demand. The deficiencies of these traditional methods become glaring when firms attempt to develop fixed fee models, capped fee structures, or alternative fee arrangements (AFAs).

Key weaknesses of Excel and legacy tools

- *No integrated historical data.* Excel cannot automatically retrieve data on similar past matters – such as final billed amounts, time spent, resource allocation, write-offs, or profitability – making every new proposal a laborious, guesswork-driven process.
- *Limited scenario modelling.* Effective pricing requires iterative "What-if?" modelling across rates, discounts, scope variations, and resourcing ratios. Spreadsheets lack the automation and flexibility for this, leaving lawyers unable to optimize profitability vs competitiveness.
- *Lack of scalability and democratization.* Perhaps most critically, spreadsheet-based solutions and even many legacy pricing platforms fail to democratize pricing expertise across the wider firm. Their functionality, complexity, and user interfaces tend to be unintuitive and unappealing to lawyers, meaning adoption is limited to a small group of pricing and commercial finance specialists. This concentration creates bottlenecks and prevents the broader partner group from engaging confidently with pricing. As a result, commercial thinking does not scale across the firm, and the pricing function remains siloed rather than embedded in everyday practice.
- *Inconsistency across partners.* Every partner's spreadsheet tends to be unique, creating a lack of pricing governance and consistency. This inconsistency not only confuses clients – who receive divergent formats, narratives, and structures – but also undermines internal alignment, making it difficult to manage margin control and profitability at scale.
- *Time-consuming.* Lawyers spend non-billable hours trawling through old files, copying content, and manually adjusting pricing elements. This inefficiency reduces time spent on value-added legal work, delays proposal turnaround, and increases the likelihood of avoidable errors.

Clients, who operate with advanced procurement and financial modelling systems, increasingly perceive manual, spreadsheet-based proposals as outdated. Worse still, spreadsheets are error-prone and difficult to update in real time, particularly when scope creep or budget overruns occur mid-matter.

When firms can only identify unprofitability after a job is completed, it's too late to intervene, resulting in write-offs and strained client relationships.

From pain point to strategic asset

Legal pricing has historically been a time-consuming, risk-laden, and low-leverage activity – often disconnected from profitability and plagued by inefficiency. Yet with the shift to hybrid service delivery, fixed fee models, and increasing client demands for transparency, pricing has become a central strategic function. Traditional tools – particularly spreadsheets and static templates – are no longer adequate. What's needed is a platform that integrates data, automation, analytics, and ease-of-use, designed with legal workflows in mind.

Virtual Pricing Director® (VPD) is one such platform. Purpose-built by lawyers for lawyers, VPD has a singular aim – to make pricing faster, smarter, more transparent, and more profitable. It is not simply a better spreadsheet – it is a complete pricing ecosystem that helps firms move from reactive, manual guesswork to confident, data-led decision-making.

Fast, high-quality proposal generation

Lawyers often view pricing as a dull, administrative task – non-billable, interruptive, and frustrating. VPD addresses this by drastically reducing the time required to build high-quality, client-ready proposals. With its generative AI scope builder, VPD can produce 85 percent of the initial draft of a pricing proposal – including assumptions and exclusions – in seconds.

Users can clone previous proposals with a single click and tailor them using intuitive dropdowns or even voice dictation. Personalized tabs like "My Favorites" and "My Recent Proposals" make it easy to retrieve trusted materials, while an advanced search function allows lawyers to instantly locate relevant past work using keywords, matter types, or client names.

Data-driven profitability forecasting

Winning the work is only half the battle. The real challenge is ensuring it's profitable. VPD continuously calculates gross profit margins in real time as the proposal is built. Lawyers can see immediately how changes in resourcing, rates, or scope affect the commercial outcome – without waiting on finance teams. This empowers fee earners to make informed pricing decisions at the point of negotiation, reducing underpricing and eliminating margin erosion.

AI-driven recommendations

Drawing from the firm's historical data, VPD can detect patterns that undermine profitability – such as underquoting, excessive write-offs, or poor scoping. Based on these insights, it can recommend proactive changes to new proposals – increasing rates, narrowing scope, altering team structure, or adjusting fee structures. These recommendations are context-specific and surfaced at the moment they are most useful – while the lawyer is still building the proposal.

Dynamic scenario modelling

One of the most powerful features of VPD is its ability to support "What if?" scenario planning. Fee earners can compare different pricing models – fixed, capped, estimate range, or hybrid – and instantly see the implications for both competitiveness and profitability. Adjustments to resource mix, discounting, or scope can be modelled in seconds, giving partners the ability to determine an optimal negotiation range ahead of client discussions.

Seamless collaboration across teams

Complex matters often require input from multiple teams or jurisdictions. VPD functions as a virtual deal room, where colleagues can contribute to shared proposals asynchronously without endless email chains or duplicated effort. This not only streamlines internal workflows but also supports multi-disciplinary, multi-office collaboration – critical for pricing large-scale or cross-border instructions.

Real-time monitoring and alerts

Pricing is not a one-off task – it is a live financial discipline. VPD includes dashboards that track budget vs actual performance at both matter and phase level. These are updated continuously – potentially every ten minutes – depending on PMS integration. Lawyers can set customised early-warning alerts for budget overruns, declining profit margins, or adverse changes in leverage. This allows them to intervene early, prevent write-offs, and preserve profitability.

To assist with client communication, VPD can also generate automated infographic reports and AI-written updates, summarizing key financials, including WIP, billing status, and variance against budget. This reduces the admin burden on lawyers while increasing transparency for clients.

Consistency, risk management, and compliance

Pricing inconsistencies across teams are a common source of risk and inefficiency. VPD addresses this with firmwide and practice group-specific libraries of standard assumptions and exclusions. These can be designated as mandatory, recommended, or optional, ensuring that proposals are legally robust and risk aligned.

VPD also integrates with Outside Counsel Guidelines (OCGs), allowing firms to automatically check proposals for potential breaches before submission. This ensures that engagements are not only commercially viable but also contractually compliant, protecting both revenue and reputation.

A strategic shift

Ultimately, VPD transforms pricing from a back-office administrative task into a core strategic function. It empowers lawyers to deliver proposals that are credible, profitable, and client friendly. It ensures pricing reflects actual costs, market conditions, and desired margin thresholds. And it creates a unified platform where pricing, monitoring, and client engagement all occur in one place – simplifying workflows while enhancing performance.

Firms that adopt tools like VPD are better equipped to compete in a world of fixed fees, subscription models, productized services, and AI-enabled delivery. Pricing becomes not a reactive chore but a forward-looking commercial capability – one that drives growth, deepens trust, and protects margin in an increasingly complex legal landscape.

Embracing the new pricing paradigm

The intersection of technology and legal pricing is the most transformative shift the profession has faced in decades. AI, automation, and productization are forcing law firms to rethink not just how they deliver services, but how they capture and communicate value. The billable hour cannot survive this new era of efficiency and transparency.

Utilizing technology is transforming the next generation of legal pricing. Not a pricing "tool" so much as a long overdue pricing, profitability, and matter management ecosystem, this type of technology is a powerful extension of a firm's practice management and document management system.

For clients, it delivers clarity, speed, and fairness. For firms, it transforms pricing from a guesswork exercise into a strategic advantage.

The future belongs to firms that embrace hybrid service delivery, fixed and subscription pricing, and productized offerings – all underpinned by robust pricing technology. Those that continue to rely on spreadsheets and intuition risk being outpaced by competitors who have mastered the art and science of value-based pricing.

Chapter 12:
Navigating legal procurement

By Steph Hogg, director of procurement consulting, Validatum

Introduction

Formalized legal procurement has long been a staple of the public sector landscape. Government departments, regulatory authorities, and public agencies have traditionally demanded a high degree of structure, transparency, and defensibility in their legal services sourcing.

This has manifested in everything from panel appointments and open tenders to detailed expressions of interest and public notices – often leaving business development, pricing, and legal teams to wrestle with the challenge of squeezing highly tailored, relationship-driven legal services into a rigid, process-heavy procurement mold. The frustration is palpable – nuance, judgement, and trust-based selling are difficult to translate into tick-box templates and fixed-price line items.

In recent years, that same structured procurement philosophy has migrated decisively into the private sector. The days when legal departments operated with relative autonomy in engaging external counsel – often based on long-standing personal relationships – are fading. Procurement, once peripheral or absent in legal spend decisions, is now a powerful and entrenched stakeholder. In many organizations, procurement has become a gatekeeper with hard-wired influence over who makes the shortlist, how value is assessed, and under what commercial and contractual terms instructions are issued.

This shift has been fueled by broader corporate priorities – cost control, vendor consolidation, ESG compliance, risk management, and the professionalization of in-house legal operations. Whether embedded within legal ops, reporting to finance, or operating as an independent sourcing function, procurement's involvement is rarely optional – even where firms enjoy strong historical ties with key decision-makers.

Law firms may find themselves blindsided by a procurement process that appears impersonal, opaque, and inflexible – with pre-defined pricing models, service level requirements, or rebate expectations that seem entirely misaligned with the realities of legal service delivery.

Yet to characterize procurement as rigid or unreasonable is to fundamentally misunderstand its role. Procurement is neither monolithic nor adversarial – but it is commercially disciplined and goal-oriented. Its mandate is typically broader than cost savings alone. It may be tasked with reducing supplier risk, increasing pricing transparency, driving innovation, or aligning external legal spend with internal business outcomes.

This chapter unpacks the inner workings of legal procurement and the mindsets that drive it. It highlights the most common missteps law firms make when engaging with procurement – from pricing proposals that fail to demonstrate value, to misjudging the metrics that matter, or alienating key stakeholders with combative or opaque responses. More importantly, it offers a playbook for engaging procurement constructively and credibly – one rooted in commercial acumen, strategic alignment, and mutual respect.

For legal pricing professionals, this is not a peripheral issue. It's a core competence. By understanding procurement's objectives, language, and levers, firms can navigate the gatekeeping function more effectively – and in doing so, not only protect margin and relationship equity, but also stand out in increasingly competitive selection processes.

Understanding legal procurement

Legal procurement often arrives shrouded in acronyms and jargon – RFP, RFI, RFQ, ITT, mini-tender, reverse auction, beauty parade, and more. While these terms are sometimes used interchangeably in practice, they each denote distinct stages of engagement, levels of commitment, and strategic intent. For example, a Request for Information (RFI) is usually exploratory – a client scoping the market, gathering intel, or mapping supplier capabilities. It's often non-binding and may never lead to formal instructions.

A Request for Proposal (RFP), by contrast, signals that the client is moving into active selection mode, typically with a set budget, deadlines, evaluation criteria, and legal needs already defined. A mini competition may take place among pre-approved panel firms, often under tight timeframes and with assumptions about baseline compliance already baked in.

Understanding not just the terminology, but the underlying intent of the exercise, is critical. A rushed response to the wrong kind of procurement process can waste valuable time and dilute pricing credibility. Equally, declining to participate without appreciating the long-game significance –

such as maintaining visibility or nurturing a nascent relationship – can be a missed opportunity. The most commercially astute law firms know how to triage incoming procurement requests – where to invest, where to test ideas, and where to politely decline.

It's easy to cast procurement as a barrier – a bureaucratic hurdle standing between lawyers and their clients. But procurement, at its core, is not designed to obstruct. Its fundamental purpose is to enforce transparency, consistency, and value in buying decisions. Especially in regulated or listed organizations, it serves a governance function – demonstrating probity, controlling cost, managing supplier risk, and ensuring that decisions are made with reference to measurable criteria rather than personality or habit.

These are entirely legitimate goals. The tension arises when the process appears to be poorly calibrated to legal services – vague scopes of work, generic evaluation rubrics, impossible word counts, and value criteria so ambiguous that they invite page-filling generalities rather than insight.

From the law firm's side, this creates a series of dilemmas. What does "value" mean in this context? Are we expected to propose innovative pricing, or stick to the client's benchmark rates? How do we differentiate ourselves meaningfully when every other firm has the same regulatory credentials, industry experience, and panel status? In the absence of clarity, many firms err on the side of caution – producing bloated, defensive responses full of generic assurances and platitudes. These rarely land well. Worse still, some firms expend considerable time and resources on submissions where they were never truly in the running, serving only to create the illusion of competition – the proverbial "stalking horse".

On the other side of the table, procurement professionals are often dealing with large volumes of supplier submissions under intense pressure from internal stakeholders. They are not lawyers, and they are not judging a submission on legal merit alone – or at all. Their lens is commercial.

They are looking for value signals – evidence of efficiency, clarity around deliverables, predictable cost structures, and mitigation of delivery risk. What they prize above all is comparability – the ability to place competing bids side by side and make a rational, defensible decision. This is why word limits, structured templates, and strict compliance with formatting rules are non-negotiable. Non-conforming responses are not seen as creative. They are seen as non-compliant.

Understanding this mindset is essential. Procurement is trained to apply discipline, not discretion. They are looking for concrete, substantiated answers – what exactly is being offered, at what price, with what measurable outcome. Claims of "excellence", "partnership", or "innovation" are ignored unless they are backed by evidence – ideally benchmarked, independently validated, or directly relevant to the client's stated goals. A law firm that responds with marketing fluff or legalese will appear tone-deaf. One that communicates with commercial clarity – tailored, concise, and outcome-focused – will stand out.

Crucially, procurement is not optional. If a client has formalized its legal services sourcing through procurement, it is a signal that the relationship is being professionalized – and that commercial rigor is now part of the engagement criteria. Attempting to bypass procurement, either by approaching in-house counsel directly or relying on informal relationships, is not only ineffective, but also reputationally damaging. It suggests a lack of respect for the client's governance processes and a failure to adapt to changing expectations. In the worst cases, it triggers internal friction between legal and procurement stakeholders, which invariably works against the firm.

The better strategy is not to resist the process, but to master it. Firms that learn the language and cadence of procurement – and tailor their submissions accordingly – will consistently outperform those that treat it as a transactional hoop to jump through. Procurement isn't going away. It's evolving. Law firms that develop the capability to respond with commercial fluency and strategic discipline will not only win more work – they will become trusted, long-term partners in the eyes of both legal and procurement teams.

Preparation starts long before the RFP

One of the most persistent and damaging myths surrounding legal procurement is the idea that the competitive process begins when the Request for Proposal (RFP) drops into your inbox. By that point, the starting gun has long since fired. The client has already defined its needs, secured internal alignment, agreed on procurement timelines, and – crucially – formed preliminary impressions about the market. In many cases, there's already an informal shortlist in play.

If your first meaningful engagement with the opportunity begins at the point of RFP release, then you are already on the back foot. You're not shaping the conversation – you're reacting to someone else's framing. And you're not building credibility – you're trying to prove it under artificial time pressure. Firms that consistently win formal tenders don't just write better responses. They embed themselves in the client's consciousness well before procurement takes the stage.

Preparation is a long game, not an event

The most effective firms treat preparation as a rolling, integrated business development discipline – not a series of one-off efforts. Success in legal procurement is cumulative. It accrues over time through repeated exposure, demonstrated expertise, and thoughtful engagement. Clients – whether consciously or subconsciously – are forming impressions well before anything is put in writing. Procurement may manage the process, but internal stakeholders influence the outcome. That means relationship-building, visibility, and positioning efforts need to begin six to 12 months in advance.

These early interactions don't need to be heavy-handed sales pitches. In fact, the most successful pre-tender engagements tend to be educational or value-based in nature – sharing insights on market trends, regulatory shifts, technology adoption, or pricing innovation. The goal is to create familiarity, build trust, and anchor your firm as a natural contender when the formal process begins.

Three dimensions of strategic preparation

Preparing effectively means planning on three fronts – internal readiness, client engagement, and intelligence gathering.

1. Internal readiness

The firms that respond quickly, confidently, and creatively to procurement exercises are the ones that have invested in internal muscle. That includes:

- *Pricing infrastructure* – rehearsed models, scenario templates, and an agreed pricing governance approach.
- *Content currency* – up-to-date, well-written case studies, credible impact metrics, and compelling evidence of value delivered.
- *Proposal agility* – systems and people capable of turning around high-quality bids under tight deadlines without panic or improvisation.

This kind of readiness isn't glamorous, but it creates a competitive edge. Clients notice the difference between a scrambled response and a disciplined one.

2. Client engagement

Procurement may control the gates, but influencers sit across the business – including general counsel, legal ops, CFOs, compliance teams, and risk officers. Are your partners developing meaningful, multidimensional relationships across those roles? Are you participating in client-hosted panels, roundtables, or advisory sessions? Have you invested in co-authoring thought leadership or providing informal guidance that doesn't come with a price tag?

The aim here is not transactional familiarity. It's to create relationship equity that will survive the scrutiny of procurement and make internal champions feel comfortable advocating for your firm during evaluation.

3. Intelligence gathering

The best bid responses feel bespoke because they are rooted in genuine understanding. That insight doesn't appear by magic. It comes from proactive intelligence gathering:

- Reviewing prior RFPs or tender results (if publicly available or shared by other contacts).
- Identifying key themes in post-tender feedback – why did you win or lose last time?
- Understanding the client's broader commercial strategy, cost pressures, ESG priorities, or digital transformation goals.

Some firms take this a step further by conducting pre-mortems – asking in advance, *If we lose this bid, what will have caused it?* – and then using that reverse logic to proactively close credibility gaps.

Pre-positioning content and narrative

Another common trait among consistently successful firms is the development of modular, reusable content – but with a twist. Rather than generic boilerplate, they curate and segment material by sector, buyer persona, and service line. This means that when an RFP does emerge, the firm is not starting from zero – it is simply tailoring an already robust narrative to fit the procurement frame.

Equally important is narrative cohesion. Winning submissions aren't just a string of answers – they're a story. *Why us? Why now? Why this team?* That story should be in the client's mind before it reads your RFP response. The submission itself should feel like a confirmation of existing trust – not a cold pitch.

Winning is about preparedness, not just responsiveness

At the end of the day, the firms that consistently win competitive tenders don't just write sharper answers or quote lower fees. They arrive better prepared. They anticipate. They shape. They embed. By the time the RFP is issued, they're not just another bidder – they're the logical choice. It's worth remembering that in legal procurement, as in life, first impressions are rarely made on the first day.

Step 1: Assess the opportunity

Too often, law firms respond to tenders with a knee-jerk yes – driven by fear of missing out, internal pressure to "go for everything", or misplaced optimism. But every RFP is not a real opportunity. Some are formalities, others are fishing expeditions, and a few are traps that can quietly erode margin, morale, or both.

The most effective firms meet each tender with disciplined curiosity. Instead of reacting, they interrogate. What is the client actually trying to achieve? Is this a commodity purchase, a cost challenge, or a strategic partnership in disguise? And, crucially, is this a fight worth entering?

Ask yourself:
- Is the work repeatable, scalable, and profitable, or is it one-off and high-risk?
- Are you the incumbent, disruptor, or decoy?
- Does the client want genuine innovation, or is it simply trying to apply pricing pressure to the status quo?
- What's the power dynamic between procurement, legal, and the business? Is there internal sponsorship for your firm?

Critically, you must be willing to say no – and say it well. A respectful, well-framed withdrawal not only preserves relationships, it can enhance credibility. It signals strategic clarity and commercial maturity. And it protects internal resources from being burned on a bid you were never likely to win or couldn't afford to deliver.

Step 2: Triage the opportunity

Triage transforms gut feel into a structured, repeatable decision framework. It allows firms to prioritize smartly, not just reactively. Without triage, you risk spreading your best people thin across low-value tenders while missing high-value ones that truly deserve your A-team.

Build a triage matrix that evaluates each opportunity against key dimensions:

- *Strategic alignment.* Does the work advance your firm's goals in terms of sector dominance, geographic footprint, or growth priorities?
- *Relationship depth.* Are there warm relationships, or is this a cold entry?
- *Revenue vs profitability.* Will this be worth winning, not just billing?
- *Delivery complexity and risk.* Does your team have capacity, capability, and appetite?
- *Compliance burden.* Is the required onboarding and MI/reporting sustainable?
- *Opportunity cost.* What are you giving up to pursue this?

Table 1: Red flags to watch for.

Red flag	What it might indicate
No scoring matrix	Opaque decision-making or pre-selected winner
>10 firms invited	Token competition to drive down pricing
Flat rates locked for 3+ years	High exposure to inflation or scope creep
No clarification window	Closed-door process, limited room for influence

Even when red flags appear, they aren't always disqualifying. A smartly worded clarification request can neutralize ambiguity, reposition value, or expose scope gaps others miss.

Strategic withdrawal

A regional firm received a tender for employment advice with aggressive demands: 20 percent fee reduction, 72-hour SLAs, and unlimited MI reporting. Internal modelling revealed a projected 16 percent loss margin. Rather than bid out of fear, the firm invoked the triage matrix, politely declined, and offered future project-based support. Six months later, the client returned – awarding the firm a high-margin workplace investigation matter. Sometimes, "no" is the smartest option.

Step 3: Responding to questions

The questions in a tender aren't just administrative hurdles – they're signposts to the client's priorities. Each response should be a mini-business case – concise, tailored, and anchored in the evaluation criteria. If scoring criteria are published, make them your North Star. If not, work to the common five Cs: Capability, Capacity, Commerciality, Client Care, and Cost Management.

Shift from claim to proof

Too many submissions rely on hollow assertions and overused phrases. Elevate your response from claim to credible evidence.

- Generic: "We have deep experience in banking litigation."
- Credible: "Over the past 12 months, we advised five FTSE 250 banks across 24 litigation matters, achieving pre-trial resolution in 83 percent of cases and saving clients £8.4m in projected legal costs."

Use:

- Measurable outcomes.
- Industry-specific examples.
- Independent rankings or testimonials.
- Client quotes (with permission).

Clarify to win

A tech-focused firm received an RFP for flat-fee patent filings – with no volume or jurisdiction data. Most firms guessed and submitted bids based on averages. One firm sought clarification, proposing three fee models based on assumed volume and complexity bands. Procurement revised the RFP and ultimately awarded the work to the firm that asked the smart question. Curiosity beats compliance.

Step 4: Financial response

This is often the make-or-break moment. You're not just quoting a number – you're signaling how well you understand the work, your commercial discipline, and your appetite for risk.

Procurement wants:

- Sustainable pricing – not a "win today, renegotiate tomorrow" model.
- Evidence of scope understanding – alignment between what's priced and what's expected.
- Clear risk allocation – how will you deal with overrun, delay, or ambiguity?

Table 2: Applying the Kraljic Matrix.

Work type	Strategic importance	Risk level	Suggested pricing approach
Routine contracts	Medium	Low	Fixed fee with volume bands and assumptions
Complex investigations	High	High	Blended rates with contingency or risk premium
Regulatory compliance	High	Medium	Retainer with milestone-linked payments
HR advice	Low	Low	Hourly or capped, with service-level triggers

Beware round-number discounts

A flat ten percent discount raises red flags – it looks arbitrary. A 7.6 percent discount, on the other hand, suggests modelling rigor. It signals that you've actually costed delivery, allowed for margin, and considered scope variability. Precision breeds credibility.

Step 5: Negotiation

This is where discipline matters most. Procurement may push hard – citing competitor rates, internal benchmarks, or perceived market norms. But you're not just selling price. You're offering value underpinned by confidence and commercial clarity.

Ask smart questions:

- Who are the comparators? Are they like-for-like in scope, geography, and expertise?
- What assumptions are being made about seniority, availability, or turn-around time?

When pressured on price, offer conditional value trades instead:

- Faster payment terms.

- Longer contract tenure.
- Scope clarity or limitations.
- Reduced reporting or onboarding requirements.
- Off-peak resourcing models.

Your goal isn't to win a race to the bottom – it's to frame yourself as a disciplined, commercially fluent partner who understands the rules and knows how to play strategically.

Step 6: Prepare for the next tender

World-class firms treat every tender – win or lose – as market research in disguise. The end of a process is the beginning of the next one. A rigorous post-mortem is where real improvement happens.

Best-in-class firms:

- Log every evaluation score (win or lose).
- Capture debrief feedback – including informal procurement comments.
- Identify recurring client priorities – e.g. diversity, tech enablement, ESG.
- Debrief internally – with partners, pricing, BD, and delivery teams.
- Update playbooks – with refined boilerplate, case studies, and objections handling.

Turning loss into win

A mid-tier firm failed to retain its panel place after scoring poorly on tech enablement and diversity. Instead of walking away, it invested in new dashboards, ran internal inclusion workshops, and hired a client success lead. At the next refresh, it didn't just improve – it won the full mandate.

Feedback is not criticism. It's free consulting. Use it.

Procurement as partner

Procurement is often cast – wrongly – as the antagonist in the law firm–client relationship. In this caricature, procurement is cost-obsessed, indifferent to nuance, and blind to the human dimension of legal service delivery. But this view is not only outdated – it's commercially self-defeating.

Procurement is not anti-lawyer. It is not anti-margin. What it is – resolutely – is anti-ambiguity. It seeks clarity where lawyers often trade in complexity. It values comparability where law firms may default to storytelling. And it prizes discipline over improvisation. This is not adversarial. It's a different language – and one that commercially astute firms must learn to speak fluently.

The firms that win more often – and more profitably – don't necessarily offer the lowest fees. They offer the clearest narrative, the most credible evidence, and the most thoughtful commercial logic. They know what they're good at, they know what it costs to deliver, and they communicate both with precision. Their pricing is modelled, not guessed. Their assumptions are stated, not implied. And their responses feel consistent – not just in form, but in tone, intent, and delivery approach.

Crucially, they treat procurement with respect – not as a necessary evil or process hurdle to be tiptoed around, but as a legitimate, strategic client stakeholder. They engage early, respond coherently, negotiate intelligently, and follow through with professionalism. They understand that procurement is often the client's proxy for risk management, budget discipline, and internal accountability – not a barrier, but a bridge to sustained commercial engagement.

In a market where law firms are increasingly interchangeable in credentials, capability, and coverage, the differentiator is often commercial fluency. Procurement isn't the problem. In many cases, it's the opportunity – a clear-headed, business-minded ally in a world of growing client scrutiny and cost consciousness.

The future of legal procurement is not less involvement – it's more. More influence, more sophistication, and more expectations. Law firms that embrace this reality, that adapt to its rhythm and requirements, will not only win more work – they will win the right work. Work that aligns with their strengths, supports margin integrity, and builds trust across both legal and commercial stakeholders.

Don't try to outmaneuver procurement. Partner with it. Understand its incentives. Respect its process. Communicate like a business – not just a profession. Procurement is no longer the gatekeeper to be bypassed. It's the bridge to long-term, profitable, sustainable work. Cross it wisely – and with purpose.

Chapter 13:
Measuring success – metrics and KPIs for legal pricing models

By Tanbir Jasimuddin, freelance finance and analytics transformation director

The importance of measuring performance – "what gets measured, gets done"

Despite the unknown origins of this particular cliché, getting performance measurement right is critical to successful business outcomes. Clearly defined measures that link to strategic objectives and cascade throughout the organization ensure that everyone is incentivized to work together towards a common goal.

We see many firms set billable hours targets for their fee earners. This encourages fee earners to record as much time as possible, regardless of value to the client and, more importantly, recoverability. Firms that switch measures to cash collected and matter profitability will experience significantly less dysfunctional behaviors.

In my previous chapter, I discussed how legal pricing is increasing in complexity. We now need to ensure that pricing decision-makers:

- Are suitably incentivized to make pricing decisions that benefit both the firm and their clients; and
- Have insights into how effective their pricing decisions are so that they can course-correct if required.

In this chapter, I explore the thought process behind creating measures that drive congruent and profitable behaviors, and then go on to suggest types of analyses that a law firm can perform to ascertain the relative performance of pricing initiatives.

Building and deploying analytics platforms is a book in its own right. The specifics of implementation will not be covered in this chapter.[1]

KPIs vs metrics

Unfortunately, it is all too common for law firm finance teams to produce monthly reports containing several hundred key performance indicators

(KPIs). If you are reporting several hundred, they are not "key". In reality, these firms report what is known as "Result Indicators" and these RIs detract focus from the true KPIs. Whilst the analysis teams think they are helping the firm, their impact is the opposite.

A typical organization will only have a handful of KPIs. These point towards actions where, if you get it right, pretty much everything else in the organization falls into place. A famous example is British Airways during its turnaround phase in the 1980s. BA reportedly focused on just a single KPI – whether or not an aircraft takes off or lands on time.[2] Achieving this "on time performance" would result in lower airport charges, simplified airport operations, less chance of losing baggage, and satisfied customers. Measuring this KPI focused the efforts of all those involved to ensure that the aircraft did indeed take off and land on time.

In contrast to this example, most law firms use "lagging" indicators such as profit per equity partner (PEP). Whilst important, these metrics are the result of performance, not the drivers of it. Forward-looking indicators in a law firm will be a variation of the following:

- Realized price per hour.
- Utilization percent.
- Realization percent (also known as recovery rate percent).

Monitoring these performance measures allows you to "course correct" long before the PEP is known.

Value drivers and the business model of a law firm

The reason for the existence of most organizations is to create economic value for their owners. In the context of a publicly traded organization, this is termed "shareholder value". For a law firm, the equivalent is "equity partner value".

Alfred Rappaport's seminal work in 1986, *Creating Shareholder Value*, defined seven drivers of organizational value[3] that generate long-term value for firm owners. These value drivers (Figure 1) can be influenced directly by firm management through both strategic and operational decisions. This forms the foundation of much of our present day thinking on designing organizational performance management systems.

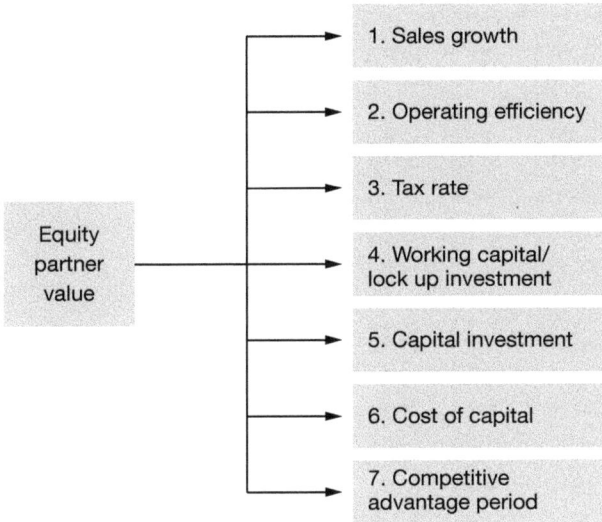

Figure 1: Rappaport's seven organizational value drivers.

We can take the core aspects of the value drivers framework and apply it to a law firm. This is a model that is often referred to as the value leakage model (Figure 2). The beauty of this model is its simplicity. It defines six groups of interventions a management team can action to improve firm profitability.

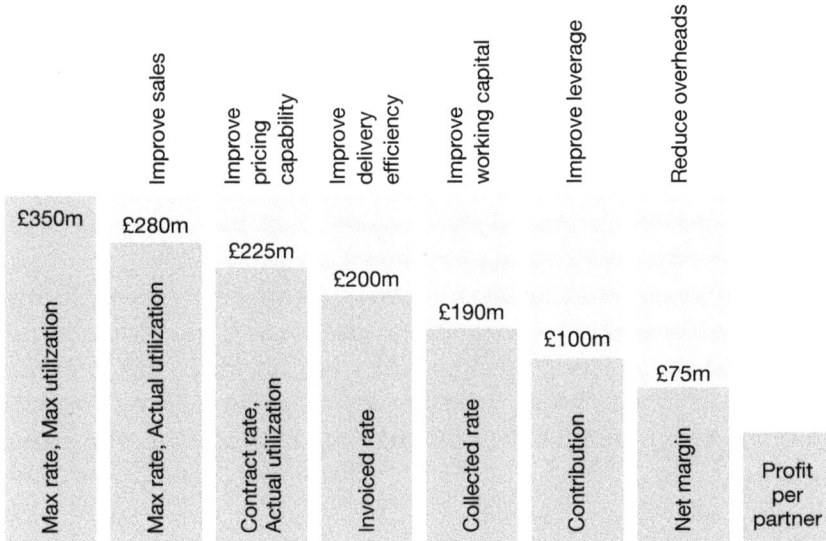

Figure 2: Value drivers in a law firm.

Starting on the left-hand side:

- We calculate the maximum possible revenue of a firm. This is the total fee earner capacity multiplied by the maximum fee earner charge out rates.
- Next, we calculate actual chargeable hours worked multiplied by the maximum possible rate. The management action to minimize the value between the two bars is to sell more (i.e. increase chargeable hours). This can be done by:
  - Selling more to existing clients (i.e. cross-selling).
  - Converting new clients.
- Then we calculate actual utilization multiplied by contracted rates. The difference here represents the average discount applied to rate cards. The management action here is to ensure fee earners can improve their pricing skills.
- The next bar is what has been billed, after write-offs (i.e. billing recovery percent). This represents the operating efficiency.
- Then we have what we have actually collected – this is about lock up management.
- Next we have operating margin. This can be influenced by the team structure and how the work is allocated.
- The next bar represents management of overheads, and finally we are left with profits available for distribution.

The importance of this framework is that it clearly defines the actions the management team can take, and we can assign a KPI or a metric next to each one of these actions to monitor how effective these actions are. Even more critical is that it focuses analytics only on the metrics that make a difference. With this model, you can explain a firm's performance with 10 to 15 dashboards – a far cry from the 250-page report!

One observation here in relation to pricing is that, while we are moving towards value-based pricing models, the operations of the firm are still people- and capacity-based. There may be scenarios where you employ a flexible workforce and only pay them for value delivered to clients. However, the reality is most firms will still employ staff on a full-time basis. This makes it a challenge to price based on value but manage firm operations with the traditional chargeable hours model.

I have covered the core aspects of performance analytics theory. In the following sections, I will apply these principles to developing pricing KPIs and metrics.

Defining the measures of performance

Referencing the framework in Figure 2, let's focus on the Price better / Improve pricing capability drivers. We will also look at how to develop metrics to measure the effectiveness of pricing strategies.

Analytics should never be siloed. You cannot analyze financial data on its own. Context is key. You need to look at all of the information together to piece together what is really going on. Therefore, when reviewing pricing performance, you need to review three categories of information:

1. *Financial indicators.* "Is this pricing strategy profitable and financially sustainable?"
2. *Client-centric indicators.* "Does this pricing strategy deliver value to a client and help develop long-lasting relationships?"
3. *Operational indicators.* "Are our internal processes optimized to meet client expectations and deliver profitability within this pricing model?"

Jim Collins states that good-to-great transformations do not happen in one go. The process of improvement relies on "relentlessly pushing a flywheel" until you start to build momentum and breakthrough.[4]

Similarly, the three pricing pillars should be viewed as part of a "flywheel of pricing performance", working together to create positive momentum. The starting point could be an investment in operational efficiency to allow the firm to work faster and at a lower internal cost. This will allow the firm to offer profitable AFAs. The cost predictability and perceived fairness will lead to improved client satisfaction and therefore strengthen long-term relationships. This will lead to improved long-term revenue growth and financial performance. This will allow further investment into operational efficiency, and so the cycle starts again.

Financial indicators

- *Realized price per hour.* This is calculated by dividing total collected income by total number of billable hours worked. This is a KPI. It is an indicator of true profitability of a firm as it reflects the impact of discounts and write-offs.
- *Matter profitability.* This is calculated by attributing fee earner costs to revenues generated by the matter. By calculating profitability at a matter level, a firm can deduce the types of work, clients, and fee arrangements that generate the most value and the ones that are

accretive. McKinsey's recommended approach is based on granular, transaction-level analytics to identify sources of margin leakage. Breaking down and analyzing the segments at granular levels allows you to correlate the factors involved in either profitability (e.g. if the fee arrangement was priced correctly, or if client demand eroded the profitability of an otherwise profitable work stream).

- *Revenue per lawyer.* This is calculated by dividing the total income by the number of lawyers. This metric is an indicator of pricing perform-ance at a macro level. A consistently high value is an indicator of a firm's ability to achieve a higher value for its services.
- *Collection rate.* This is calculated by dividing the total income by the number of lawyers. This metric is an indicator of pricing performance at a macro level. A consistently high value is an indicator of a firm's ability to achieve a higher value for its services
- *Lock up days.* This is calculated by dividing the total income by the number of lawyers. This metric is an indicator of pricing performance at a macro level. A consistently high value is an indicator of a firm's ability to achieve a higher value for its services.

Client centric metrics

- *Net Promoter Score (NPS).* This is calculated by subtracting the number of detractors from the number of promoters. This metric helps answer the question, "Are our clients loyal advocates? Or are we at risk of losing them?"
- *Client Satisfaction Score (CSAT).*[5] Collected from survey data, this is calculated by dividing the number of satisfied clients by the number of respondents. It is good practice to deploy regular, short surveys – often after key milestones. Using a small number of targeted questions, especially around billing transparency and value delivered, you will uncover what the client is really feeling.
- *Client retention rate.* This is calculated by dividing total collected income by total number of billable hours worked. This is a KPI. It is an indicator of true profitability of a firm as it reflects the impact of discounts and write-offs.
- *Referral rate.* This is calculated by dividing total collected income by total number of billable hours worked. This is a KPI. It is an indicator of true profitability of a firm as it reflects the impact of discounts and write-offs.

Operational efficiency metrics

- *Utilization rate.* This is calculated by dividing the billable hours worked by the total available hours. This is a KPI. It is an indicator of how busy the fee earners are. With the increase in AFAs, the context of this KPI needs to be monitored carefully. We want to encourage efficiency rather than time dumping. Therefore, it needs to be viewed alongside realization percent and client satisfaction scores.
- *Case cycle time.* Average elapsed time from matter opening to matter closing. This shows how efficient a firm is at delivering its services and where there could be bottlenecks.

Joining the dots

At a global soft drinks manufacturer, we observed two senior-level meetings. In the first, the daily volumes numbers were analyzed and there was doom and gloom as the numbers were falling. In the second meeting, the market share numbers, covering the same period, were discussed. There were high-fives as they saw a positive impact of their marketing campaigns and gained market share over their competitors. Was it right that one meeting was gloomy, and the other upbeat? If they analyzed both sets of data together the answer would have been somewhere in between, with a more pragmatic outcome.

Similarly, in law, it is essential to analyze client sentiment alongside financial profitability. We need to understand the answers to critical questions. Are we profitable because our clients are happy? Or in spite of them being unhappy? Are our most profitable clients the happiest? Here are a few analyses that you can perform to help answer these questions.

Analysis 1: How does the realization rate correlate with client satisfaction? (a leading indicator of churn)

Whilst there are many factors that impact realization rate, one scenario is a client who is unhappy with the value they think they are getting. This leads to constant cost challenges and ultimately write offs. These behaviors impact realization rate long before any survey results. Therefore, monitoring realization rate, and the underlying reasons, is critical to understanding client perception and the likelihood of churn. Over time, firms should continually plot this financial metric (realization rate) vs client satisfaction metrics. The data can be used to cluster clients into a 2x2 matrix, and make appropriate interventions, as seen in Figure 3.

Net promoter score

Low   High

Realization rate

High

Ticking time bombs   **Star clients**

At risk   **Crowd pleasers**

Low

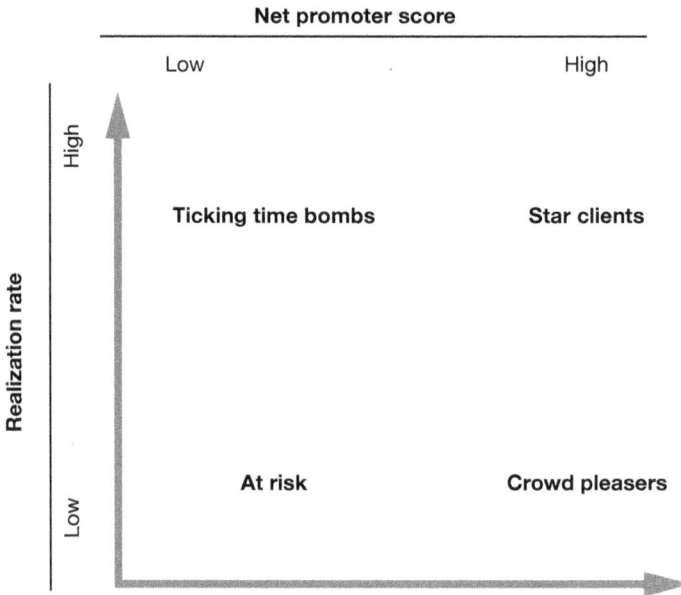

Figure 3: Realization vs NPS.

- *Star clients.* In the ideal scenario, you want to ensure that the majority of your clients are in the top right – Realization and NPS are both high. Your firm is profitable, and the client perceives the value they are receiving as fair.
- *Crowd pleasers.* Despite the clients appearing to be happy, the relationship is unprofitable owing to excessive discounting and write-offs. In this case, intervention is required to manage the relationship with the client to ensure that they see the value delivered to them.
- *Ticking time bombs.* Whilst the relationship is profitable, the client does not see the value they are receiving. Unless this is discussed with them, they are at high risk of churn.
- *At risk.* Neither the client nor the firm is happy in this instance. The firm must make a decision to either repair the relationship or stop working for the client.

This matrix provides a framework to help prioritize actions towards building a healthy and profitable relationship with the client.

Analysis 2: Are your happiest clients the most profitable?

Let us segment this analysis further. We will keep NPS but replace Realization with Matter Profit Margin. Why didn't we do this to start with?

- Realization rate is a readily available and understood metric in law firms.
- Many firms do not have the capability to define and measure profitability at a matter level.

Therefore, analysis using realization is a useful starting point. However, segmenting further using matter profitability can uncover more insights into client behaviors, and identify the relationships that really are the most valuable.

For example, you could find clients with a high NPS. However, they could be "high maintenance" and consistently requiring the firm to go above and beyond – eroding profitability. Conversely, you could have profitable clients who are passive / low touch. They may be happy, but they are at risk of being poached.

This deeper level of analysis provides useful insights into which clients are the most valuable and the ones you should invest in.

Analysis 3: How does the AFA perform vs the billable hour?

The reason firms want to pursue AFAs are:

- We will improve long-term retention of clients by offering greater cost predictability.
- If we can work more efficiently, AFAs will be more profitable than the billable hour.

The law firm needs to set up continuous monitoring to ensure that these objectives are being delivered. The performance of AFAs should be monitored against the billable hour equivalent. The measures to monitor should include:

- *Profit margin per matter.* Is the firm adequately scoping / pricing its fixed fee work?
- *Realization rate.* Does the work stay within scope?
- *Lockup days.* Do the clear terms of an AFA lead to faster billing and payment cycles compared to hourly bills (which are more prone to disputes)?
- *Post-matter completion client feedback scores.* Are clients happier, especially with the increased cost predictability?

These analyses will allow the firm to achieve a data-informed view of the impact of AFAs, and highlight areas where they could improve.

McKinsey advocates segmenting the analysis further.[6] Its approach requires using analytics to determine price sensitivity across different groups, such as:

- Key value items – high sensitivity, requiring competitive pricing.
- Foreground items – mid sensitivity.
- Background items – low sensitivity, offering margin opportunities.

In the legal sector, routine services could fall under "key value items" categories, which need to be priced competitively to attract clients. This could be balanced with highly bespoke advisory services where the price is not as much of a concern for the client. This granular segmentation allows for a more nuanced and profitable pricing strategy across the portfolio.

So far, we have covered the types of measures to monitor and the types of analyses to perform to understand how the firm is performing on both pricing and its AFAs. However, bringing the data to the decision-makers is only part of the challenge. To drive improvements in performance, you need to ensure that the data is being acted upon.

Embedding governance and discipline

A well-known food retailer wanted to understand how to reduce waste. As it predominantly stocked fresh food, it needed to understand the demand for each item, and therefore how much it needed to stock for its busy periods. It wanted to understand this at store level. A data science team had identified several hundred "demand signals" for each store location. This allowed them to accurately predict how much stock was needed to meet localized demand. However, there was no improvement in the company's waste issues. The reason was that the store managers were responsible for ordering stock, and they ignored the data they were presented with – some because they didn't understand the data and others because they thought they knew better. It is a well-known cliché that two-thirds of any data project needs to be spent on changing behaviors. This is even harder in a law firm, where your stakeholders are not only highly intelligent, but also highly trained to argue with you.

Change management is an academic discipline in its own right. Ever since the days of Kotter and Lewin in the 1980s, significant research has gone into this, and there are well-trodden playbooks to deliver change.

One of the biggest challenges is that lawyers are not incentivized sufficiently to adopt better financial discipline – including AFAs. The law firm needs to build a data culture.

Firstly, a clear message needs to come from the top – data analytics and pricing is critical not only to long-term growth, but the ability to outperform competitors.

Secondly, partners need to be incentivized to deliver on financial metrics – a surprisingly large number of firms do not do this, and the partners have no incentive to adopt new pricing approaches.

Thirdly, partners need to be trained to shift their client conversations away from a narrow focus on hourly rates towards a broader discussion of value, scope and outcomes. This involves teaching partners to:

- Conduct scoping conversations with clients to understand their objectives and what a successful outcome looks like from their point of view.
- Clearly articulate the value proposition behind a proposed fee, linking the price to a specific outcome that will be delivered.
- Present a range of pricing options, allowing the client to choose the one that is most appropriate for their needs.
- Proactively manage scope and be transparent when circumstances require a change in the initial fee quotation.

Allied to this, partners need to adopt a value-selling mindset. McKinsey emphasizes the importance of building skills and confidence among the front line[7] – in a law firm, this is the lawyers / partners who must negotiate and justify fees. Confidence and empowerment will require trustworthy analytics that they can navigate. A focus on these capabilities will ensure that data-informed pricing becomes embedded.

Lastly, the firm needs to embrace a culture of measurement and transparency. The firm needs to foster a culture where strategic decisions are based on facts and objective analysis, not intuition or gut feel. The right KPIs, visible in near-real-time, will create a culture of accountability, where every firm member will understand their role in driving value.

Conclusions

When done right, measuring performance and profitability is a win-win for all. This is not an easy journey. Firms will need to unlearn bad habits before building new ones.

The principles presented in this chapter will help you focus on metrics that truly matter. The drivers of profitability presented are not corporate abstract concepts, but ones that will help define the KPIs that govern performance. They will also help guide actions that will improve long-term profitability.

However, this is not just an analytics exercise. It requires a fundamental shift in culture and mindset, enabled by the deployment of technology.

References

1   https://fpa-trends.com/sites/default/files/docs/FPA-Trends-Insights-Paper-2024-Mastering-Data-In-FPA.pdf
2   www.scribd.com/document/638807898/5-An-Airplane-KPI-Case-docx
3   https://www.oxfordreference.com/view/10.1093/oi/authority.20110803115134707
4   www.jimcollins.com/concepts/the-flywheel.html
5   www.legal500.com/faqs-single/what-criteria-makes-up-a-client-satisfaction-score/
6   www.mckinsey.com/capabilities/growth-marketing-and-sales/our-insights/pricing-and-promotions-the-analytics-opportunity
7   www.mckinsey.com/capabilities/growth-marketing-and-sales/our-insights/ebook-the-hidden-power-of-pricing-how-b2b-companies-can-unlock-profit#/

Chapter 14:

The future of legal services pricing – what do the next five years hold?

By Richard Burcher, founder and managing director, Validatum®, and founder and CEO, Virtual Pricing Director®

Pricing at a crossroads

Legal services pricing is undergoing a profound and unavoidable transformation. What was once considered a mechanical afterthought to service delivery is now recognized as a strategic capability – one that directly influences profitability, client trust, market positioning, and competitive advantage. In many firms, the way pricing is approached today still bears the hallmarks of legacy practice – time-based billing, retrospective scoping, and a narrow focus on input rather than impact. But across the profession, there is a growing realization that pricing is no longer just a technical function. It is a commercial imperative.

This inflection point has not emerged in a vacuum. It is the product of a perfect storm – increasing client price sensitivity and procurement sophistication, economic uncertainty and inflationary cost pressures, margin compression, talent expectations for more purposeful work, and the inexorable rise of technology, from AI to workflow automation to predictive analytics.

Clients are demanding more, faster, and at greater value. In-house legal teams, emboldened by legal operations and procurement professionals, powerful data, and outside counsel management software, are pushing for alternative fee arrangements, fixed budgets, and greater transparency, not as a favor, but as a precondition for continued engagement.

For law firms, this moment presents both a threat and an opportunity. Those who cling to outdated models risk commoditization, write-downs, and exclusion from increasingly strategic client mandates. Those who embrace pricing innovation stand to differentiate themselves not just on service quality, but on commercial acumen, strategic alignment, and business empathy. Pricing, in this new world, becomes a lens through which clients assess whether a firm understands their reality and whether it is capable of helping them navigate it.

Importantly, this transformation is not just about changing numbers on a page. It requires changes in mindset, skillset, infrastructure, governance, and behavior. It touches everything from how matters are scoped and resourced to how lawyers talk about value and risk with clients. The shift challenges long-held assumptions about what constitutes merit, value, and success within law firms and demands a new language of commercial fluency and trust-building.

This chapter takes the position that the next five years will see a radical redefinition of legal services pricing. Some of the shifts will be incremental and already underway, others will be structural and cultural, and a few will be imaginative and game changing.

Taken together, they will redraw the landscape on which firms compete and collaborate. The purpose of this chapter is not to predict the future in generalities, but to provide a strategic roadmap for progressive firms willing to lead. It explores not only what is likely to happen, but why, and what it will mean for the architecture, culture, and relationships that define the modern legal business.

The next five years – from safe bets to stretch bets

When looking ahead to the future of legal services pricing, the question is not whether change will occur, but rather how far it will go, and how quickly. Some of the change is already happening around us – the decline of hourly billing, the rise of pricing professionals, the increasing adoption of pricing technology.

These are the safe bets – predictable, incremental evolutions that reflect growing maturity in the discipline. But beyond the visible horizon lies a more disruptive set of possibilities – AI-driven pricing automation, client self-service interfaces, outcome-based commercial partnerships, and even autonomous negotiation between legal bots and client systems. These are the stretch bets – less certain, but potentially transformative.

To make sense of this range, we propose a "three-horizon framework" as a way to structure the conversation. This model distinguishes between:

- *Horizon one – the obvious and overdue.* These are the pricing improvements already underway, where the primary challenge is execution, not vision. They include the adoption of fixed fees, increased use of technology, more robust profitability metrics, and better governance structures.
- *Horizon two – structural and cultural rewiring.* These changes involve

deeper rethinking of organizational behavior, partner incentives, pricing narratives, and the professional identity of lawyers as commercial actors. Success here depends as much on internal belief systems as on external tools.

- *Horizon three – radical innovation and imaginative disruption.* This horizon looks at emerging possibilities that may seem bold – or even far-fetched – but are increasingly feasible given current trends in AI, data, and service design. It is where pricing becomes a product, an experience, or an autonomous system.

This framework allows us to explore the future not as a binary of the plausible versus the fantastical, but as a spectrum of evolution, each stage building upon the one before. It invites firms to assess where they currently sit – not just in terms of tools or processes, but in ambition, capability, and mindset.

A firm may be advanced in Horizon one (e.g., using sophisticated pricing platforms) but underdeveloped in Horizon two (still rewarding hours over outcomes), or entirely unprepared for Horizon three (where clients want licensable knowledge tools, not just legal advice).

It also forces an uncomfortable but necessary truth – the gap between the best and the rest is widening. The most innovative firms are no longer simply responding to pricing pressure – they are using pricing strategy as a proactive lever for market differentiation, value creation, and long-term client intimacy and dependence. Meanwhile, firms that treat pricing as a compliance issue or an internal administrative burden are being quietly but steadily disqualified from serious client consideration.

By organizing the chapter around these three horizons, we aim to give firms a way to think about pricing maturity, not just in terms of inputs or outcomes, but in terms of trajectory. The question becomes not just, "Are we doing this well now?" but "How well are we positioned for what's next?".

Each horizon requires different capabilities, different conversations, and different types of courage. Horizon one is about discipline and process, Horizon two is about culture and accountability, and Horizon three is about vision and experimentation. This chapter will explore all three in turn, offering insight into what they involve, why they matter, and what practical steps firms can take to move forward.

Horizon one – the obvious and overdue

For many firms, the future of pricing doesn't begin with radical transformation – it begins with long-overdue correction. Horizon one represents the low-hanging fruit – the commercial and operational improvements that firms have long acknowledged as necessary but often failed to implement consistently or with conviction. These are not ideas on the fringe. They are increasingly mainstream expectations, both from clients and from a growing cohort of commercially minded lawyers and senior law firm leaders and business professionals. Their implementation is no longer a differentiator – it's a baseline.

The decline of the hourly rate as default

The most visible shift is the continued erosion of time-based billing as the default model. While hourly rates will not disappear entirely and nor should they, in some contexts they are being displaced across a growing range of work types by fixed, capped, retainer, subscription, and risk-sharing arrangements. Clients now expect budget predictability, pricing transparency, and meaningful value articulation. For commoditized or high-volume work, the hourly rate has become commercially and politically untenable.

This shift is most obvious in areas like employment, real estate, regulatory compliance, and commercial contracts, but it is also creeping into advisory and disputes work, particularly for phases that can be clearly scoped. For firms, this means developing clearer scoping processes, better data on historical delivery costs, and the ability to structure pricing around deliverables rather than effort. That requires tools, training, and a mindset shift from billing time to selling value.

The rise of procurement and legal operations

The growing influence of procurement and legal operations has added further rigor to the pricing conversation. These professionals are data-literate, KPI-driven, and commercially fluent and they expect law firms to engage on those same terms. They benchmark fees across panels, apply pricing pressure with surgical precision, and increasingly favor firms that can demonstrate pricing governance, consistency, and transparency.

What once felt like a nuisance is now a non-negotiable feature of the modern client landscape. Firms that treat procurement as an obstacle rather than a partner risk alienating decision-makers and losing access to strategically important work. The firms that thrive in this environment are those that come to the table with structured pricing methodologies, robust commercial narratives, and the confidence to explain – not just justify – their fees.

Technology – from spreadsheet to platform

Another overdue but essential shift is the replacement of spreadsheets and email chains with dedicated pricing platforms. Tools like Virtual Pricing Director® allow lawyers to scope work, run pricing scenarios, generate proposals, forecast profitability, and monitor performance in real time. These are no longer nice-to-haves. In a world of compressed margins and rapid turnaround expectations, the ability to price accurately, efficiently, and at scale is a commercial imperative.

What Excel lacks in structure and functionality, it makes up for in flexibility and therein lies the problem. In most firms, every partner has their own version of "how we price things", leading to inconsistency, risk, and inefficiency. Pricing platforms address this by centralizing assumptions and exclusions, enforcing governance, and making profitability insights available to lawyers at the point of pricing. They also increase partner confidence by reducing reliance on gut feel or retrospective validation from finance teams.

The adoption of these tools is not about automating judgement out of the process – it's about equipping judgement with better data, clearer logic, and faster execution. In Horizon one, the goal is not to reinvent pricing – it's to operationalize it.

The shift from revenue to profitability

A further hallmark of Horizon one maturity is the pivot from revenue growth to profit margin discipline. In many firms, revenue is still treated as the primary measure of success, even when it's decoupled from profitability. Partners win work that looks impressive on the top line but quietly bleeds margin through write-downs, overservicing, or poor scoping. Pricing strategy becomes distorted by ego, legacy client relationships, or internal competition and pricing cannibalization.

Progressive firms are challenging this by focusing on matter-level profitability, setting minimum margin thresholds, and rewarding behaviors that protect commercial sustainability. This requires integrating pricing data with matter management systems, given partners lawyer-centric financial dashboards, and building cultures where commercial fluency is seen not as a distraction from lawyering, but as an essential complement to it.

Formal pricing governance takes shape

Finally, we are seeing the institutionalization of pricing governance across a growing number of firms. This may take the form of pricing committees, deal review panels, dedicated pricing professionals, or value councils. These structures create shared accountability, offer guidance on complex deals, and ensure alignment with firm strategy. They also provide critical air cover for partners seeking to resist unnecessary discounting or to push back on unsustainable client expectations.

Importantly, governance is not about bureaucracy. It's about consistency and clarity. It allows firms to be more predictable, more transparent, and more internally aligned on what good pricing looks like. In this sense, it is both a control mechanism and a confidence booster.

In summary

Horizon one is not where innovation begins – it is where excuses end. The practices outlined here are no longer optional for firms that want to remain competitive. They are the baseline from which bolder moves can be made. Firms that fail to get serious about these foundational reforms are not only forgoing margin, but they are also signaling to clients that they are not yet fit for the modern legal marketplace.

The good news is that these reforms are entirely achievable. The tools exist. The case studies exist. The client appetite exists. What's required now is operational discipline, cultural reinforcement, and leadership commitment. Get this right, and firms build the foundation for the deeper structural rewiring and creative disruption that will define the next two horizons.

Horizon two – structural and cultural rewiring

If Horizon one is about fixing what's broken, Horizon two is about rebuilding what no longer serves. At this level, pricing transformation demands more than better tools and tighter processes – it requires rethinking the underlying structures, incentives, and behaviors that shape how legal work is valued, sold, and rewarded.

This is where the true challenge lies – the cultural and institutional architecture of many law firms was not designed for the pricing models clients now expect. And yet, it is precisely here that the most profound and enduring competitive advantages can be forged.

From pricing as admin to pricing as strategy

In many firms, pricing still sits awkwardly between finance, business development, marketing, and delivery – a reactive task that follows scoping, or worse, precedes it. To unlock sustainable improvement, pricing must become a central strategic capability – proactively planned, designed collaboratively with clients, and directly linked to both financial and service delivery goals.

This means pricing discussions taking place much earlier in the matter lifecycle, and aligning them with business development, resource planning, and client relationship management. It also means building firm-wide fluency in how pricing influences margin, effort, risk, and value perception.

In practical terms, this shift requires cross-functional collaboration between partners, pricing professionals, legal project managers, business development and finance teams. It also demands that firms articulate a clear pricing philosophy – not just a fee structure, but a commercial identity that reflects their value proposition to the market. Strategic pricing becomes a lens through which the firm expresses its differentiation and reinforces its internal discipline.

The evolution of lawyer behavior and identity

Perhaps the most difficult – but vital – shift in Horizon two is the evolution of the lawyer mindset. For generations, lawyers have been trained to avoid risk, seek certainty, and define value through technical excellence and billable time. These habits run deep. But in a pricing environment increasingly shaped by client co-design, commercial trade-offs, and business outcomes, lawyers must learn to think and behave like strategic advisors and commercial negotiators.

This requires new skills – understanding cost-to-serve, articulating value from the client's perspective, confidently discussing budget alignment and scope, and holding the line on margin when appropriate. It also requires new behaviors – collaboration, adaptability, willingness to share pricing authority, and comfort with ambiguity.

Firms that succeed in Horizon two will invest in building these capabilities through training, coaching, feedback loops, and incentives. More fundamentally, they will reframe commercial fluency not as a distraction from the practice of law, but as a defining part of 21st century professionalism.

Client collaboration – pricing as co-creation

Clients, too, are evolving. Legal operations and procurement teams are no longer satisfied with opaque quotes or "finger-in-the-air" estimates. Increasingly, they want to be active participants in pricing design – co-creating structures that reflect risk, complexity, and mutual value. This requires a new level of transparency and trust on the part of firms.

Horizon two involves embracing this co-creation ethos – working along-side clients to build pricing arrangements that align not only with budget constraints, but with broader business objectives. This may include volume-based discounts, phased delivery pricing, success-linked triggers, or embedded flexibility for scope change. What matters most is the mindset – shifting from defending fees to designing partnerships.

Done well, this approach doesn't just avoid fee disputes, it builds strategic intimacy. Pricing becomes a shared commercial language through which firm and client align expectations, manage risk, and reinforce commitment.

Challenging the sacred cows

To operate effectively at Horizon two, firms must be willing to question some of their most sacred internal practices. Chief among these is the continued reliance on time-based performance and remuneration metrics, which distort incentives and reinforce legacy behaviors. When hours billed are still the primary proxy for value – and, by extension, career progression – no amount of pricing innovation will stick.

Likewise, rigid rate structures that fail to account for matter complexity, partner leverage, or risk exposure create a false sense of fairness while under-mining profitability. Fixed internal discounting limits, artificial constraints on scope flexing, and inconsistent enforcement of pricing protocols all signal a firm not yet serious about commercial discipline.

In Horizon two, meritocracy must evolve. Performance metrics must include profitability, pricing rigor, negotiation effectiveness, and margin protection. Partner compensation systems must reward those who take commercial ownership, not just those who rack up hours or revenue. Leaders must be willing to model and reinforce these behaviors consistently across the partnership.

Redesigning internal structures and roles

As the nature of pricing evolves, so too must the organizational infrastruc-ture that supports it. This may involve the creation of new roles – pricing directors, value architects, and client commercial leads, as well as new ways of embedding pricing into matter intake, pipeline reviews, and client feedback loops. The goal is to operationalize pricing as a team sport, not a solo responsibility handed to the lead partner or delegated entirely to finance.

In mature Horizon two firms, pricing becomes a shared commercial language, supported by collaborative systems and consistent playbooks. Every partner understands their pricing guardrails, every matter team has access to profitability guidance, and every proposal benefits from both legal insight and commercial calibration.

In summary

Horizon two is where firms build the cultural and structural muscles needed for sustainable pricing evolution. It is more difficult than Horizon one because it confronts identity, hierarchy, and deeply embedded norms. It is also more powerful – the changes made here unlock not just improved commercial outcomes, but improved client trust, better team collaboration, and greater internal alignment.

Crucially, these changes are not just about coping with market pressure. They are about preparing for a world in which pricing becomes a source of competitive strength, client intimacy, and partner confidence. The firms that succeed in Horizon two will be those that treat pricing not as a compliance exercise, but as a catalyst for cultural renewal and strategic reinvention.

Horizon three – radical innovation and imaginative disruption

While Horizon one is about execution and Horizon two is about evolution, Horizon three is about reinvention. This is where pricing stops being a mirror of past practice and becomes a medium for radical transformation – of business models, client relationships, service delivery, and even the professional identity of the lawyer.

At this outer edge, we find a world shaped not only by economics and expectations, but by the accelerating potential of technology and design thinking. Although many of these innovations remain emergent, the conditions for their adoption are maturing faster than the profession anticipates.

This is not about fanciful futurism. The technologies already exist. The client appetite is already forming. The only real unknown is how willing law firms are to imagine differently, experiment bravely, and scale wisely. Horizon three invites firms to ask, "What if pricing became a platform, a product, or even a predictive service?" "What if we redefined legal pricing not as a number, but as a *commercial experience?*"

Productization of legal services

One of the most promising innovations in pricing is the productization of legal services –repackaging recurring, defined solutions into digital, licensable, or subscription-based offerings. These hybrid solutions combine legal expertise with technology, automation, and self-service tools. Once developed, they can be delivered with minimal human involvement, offering clients speed, accessibility, and affordability, while allowing firms to earn recurring, scalable revenue.

Examples already exist - digital compliance toolkits, regulatory update platforms, automated contract systems, or playbook-driven advice engines. These aren't merely tools. They're pricing assets, enabling firms to shift from charging for effort to charging for access, usage, or outcome. They also pave the way for pricing models drawn from SaaS and consulting – tiered packages, modular upgrades, freemium trials, and outcome-based pricing.

For this to take root, firms must rethink how they design, price, and deliver value. They need to move from matter-by-matter pricing to solution-centric models, supported by cross-functional teams of lawyers, technologists, and product managers. It challenges the artisan model of law, but offers significant rewards – including revenue diversity, client stickiness, and market differentiation.

AI-negotiated and dynamic pricing models

As AI advances, the potential for automated, real-time, and adaptive/ dynamic pricing becomes increasingly tangible. Imagine a world where client procurement bots interact directly with law firm pricing engines – negotiating scope, risk-sharing parameters, and delivery formats based on pre-agreed constraints, historical performance, or real-time market benchmarks.

These "AI-negotiated" pricing models would enable firms to dynamically adjust fees based on risk bands, urgency, capacity, or business outcomes. For example, a litigation matter could be priced on a dynamic risk matrix, adjusting fees as case complexity evolves. A transaction could be tied to deal value, with price variations based on milestone delivery or stakeholder satisfaction scores.

While this sounds advanced, precursors are already in play, particularly in volume-based or regulated sectors where unit cost models, performance-linked fees, and risk bands are the norm. The real leap is in making such models intelligent, adaptive, and autonomously managed. To participate in this future, firms must start building the data infrastructure and AI fluency required to support it.

Client self-service pricing interfaces

Another frontier innovation lies in client-facing pricing configurators – interactive dashboards or portals that allow clients to explore pricing options, scope variations, and delivery models in real time. Much like airline or cloud computing pricing, clients could toggle service levels, urgency, and optional add-ons, receiving instant, transparent pricing with embedded risk disclosures and profitability guardrails.

These tools offer not only pricing flexibility but client empowerment – transforming opaque, transactional conversations into co-designed commercial experiences. Clients feel in control, and firms gain efficiencies, transparency, and alignment. This demands significant design thinking and interface investment, but the result is a client journey that starts not with "How much will it cost?" but "What mix of value do I want?".

Outcome-based pricing at scale

While outcome-based pricing is not new, its scale has been limited, often confined to litigation, contingent fee models, or discrete advisory mandates. But as client demand for shared risk and aligned incentives intensifies, and as firms gain better predictive insights from AI and data, we can expect broader experimentation with pricing tied to outcomes – not inputs – across both contentious and non-contentious work.

This could mean pricing linked to business KPIs (e.g., successful regulatory approvals, reduced dispute volumes), value creation triggers (e.g., funding secured, contracts closed), or satisfaction benchmarks (e.g., user adoption, internal NPS scores). The commercial and technological complexity is high, but so too is the potential to reframe law firm value in client-centric terms.

This evolution also implies a change in posture – from fee negotiation to value alignment, from cost justification to business impact. Firms that want to lead in this space will need confidence in their data, clarity in scope, maturity in client relationships, and flexibility in delivery.

Redefining professional identity

Perhaps the most profound disruption of Horizon three is philosophical – redefining what it means to be a lawyer. As pricing becomes more productized, autonomous, and client-configured, the traditional lawyer's role shifts from drafter or negotiator to architect, curator, and strategist. Expertise is still central, but it is wrapped in service design, business fluency, and commercial imagination.

In this world, pricing is no longer an output of the legal process – it is an input into a co-designed, value-driven journey. The firms that thrive will be those that humanize technology, commercialize knowledge, and embrace experimentation, not as a threat to professionalism, but as its modern expression.

In summary
Horizon three is not for the faint-hearted. It asks firms to be bold, curious, and willing to cannibalize legacy models in pursuit of higher value. For those that step forward, the rewards are significant – new revenue streams, deeper client intimacy, competitive resilience, and internal cultural renewal.

What seems radical today will feel obvious tomorrow. The only question is who will get there first, and who will be left clinging to a pricing model that no longer matches the world around it.

Implications for law firms – adapting to a new commercial reality
The evolution of legal pricing outlined across the three horizons is not simply about new models, smarter tools, or client demands. It represents a fundamental shift in the commercial architecture of the modern law firm. Pricing no longer lives in the margins – it is moving to the center of how legal businesses win, deliver, and measure their value. For firms, this requires not just adapting to market pressure but embracing a new way of operating, thinking, and leading.

From heroes to systems
Historically, law firms have operated on a "hero model" of pricing. Senior partners, armed with deep client relationships and gut instinct, crafted pricing deals based on experience, intuition, and the art of the deal. But as pricing becomes more complex, data-driven, and multidisciplinary, this model is no longer sustainable. Firms must transition to repeatable systems, supported by robust infrastructure and collaborative teams.

This includes standardizing proposal templates, embedding pricing playbooks, integrating profitability calculators at the point of pricing, and creating automated workflows for scope, assumptions, and exclusions. It also means using technological systems not just as proposal tools, but as commercial command centers – providing real-time visibility into margins, scenarios, and risk.

The shift from hero to system doesn't diminish individual judgement – it augments it with structure, data, and support. Firms that make this shift will gain speed, consistency, and confidence. Those that don't will remain dependent on a few commercial "unicorns" while the rest of the firm drifts.

Investing in pricing capability

To lead in the new pricing landscape, firms must invest deliberately in pricing talent and roles. This includes appointing dedicated pricing professionals with commercial, financial, and behavioral expertise, elevating pricing from a back-office function to a client-facing capability, and embedding pricing accountability into partner roles, not just finance or BD.

The most progressive firms are building cross-functional pricing teams, blending legal knowledge with financial analytics, client psychology, and negotiation strategy. These teams are not just guardians of margin, they are strategic enablers, helping lawyers craft value propositions, respond to tenders, design pricing models, and manage client expectations over time.

This shift requires firms to view pricing not as an admin task, but as a strategic muscle to be developed, deployed, and refined. Like business development or knowledge management before it, pricing must become a universally recognized professional discipline – resourced, respected, and aligned with firm strategy.

Reforming partner remuneration and KPIs

Perhaps the most politically sensitive implication is the need to rethink how performance is measured and rewarded. If firms continue to incentivize individual revenue or billable hours, pricing discipline will remain elusive. True pricing maturity demands metrics and reward systems that reflect profitability, pricing quality, scope discipline, and strategic alignment.

This may include measuring partners on matter-level margin performance, adherence to pricing protocols, successful use of fixed or risk-based models, and contribution to firm-wide pricing innovation. It also means recognizing non-billable activities like proposal preparation, pricing coaching, or participation in governance bodies.

Without such reform, firms will send mixed signals – professing to value pricing discipline while rewarding behaviors that erode it. Changing KPIs and remuneration structures is difficult, but it is an essential lever for culture change and commercial alignment.

Real-time visibility and financial literacy

Another major shift is the need for real-time commercial visibility at the coalface. Partners and matter teams must be able to see, understand, and act upon financial data while scoping, pricing, and delivering work, not weeks or months after the fact.

This requires integrating pricing platforms with practice management systems, creating intuitive dashboards, and upskilling lawyers in how to interpret and use financial information. The goal is not to turn every lawyer into a finance analyst, but to build a baseline of commercial literacy – so that decisions are grounded in fact, not assumption.

This capability becomes especially vital as firms experiment with new models – fixed fees, outcome-based pricing, or subscription arrangements – where profitability is harder to track through a traditional lens. If lawyers can't see the commercial consequences of their decisions, they can't manage them.

Client-centric pricing governance

Finally, law firms must design governance structures that balance internal consistency with external responsiveness. This includes pricing committees, deal approval thresholds, and compliance with pricing guardrails, but it must also include flexibility to co-create with clients, explore new models, and learn from experimentation.

Too often, governance becomes a bottleneck, slowing down proposals or over-policing innovation. The goal is to design lightweight but effective governance, guided by principles rather than rigid rules. The best firms strike a balance – they standardize where it creates efficiency and empower where it creates value.

Crucially, governance must be client-centric, not just risk-averse. It must consider what pricing models support deeper relationships, enhance trust, and deliver sustainable outcomes – not just what protects margin today. This mindset shift from internal control to client partnership is subtle, but trans-formative.

In summary

The implications of modern pricing for law firms are far-reaching. It's not just about changing how matters are priced – it's about re-engineering how commercial value is defined, delivered, and rewarded across the firm. It touches strategy, culture, infrastructure, talent, and leadership.

Firms that succeed in this transformation will be those that embrace commercial maturity without losing their professional soul – that blend systems with judgment, discipline with creativity, and profitability with client intimacy. They will move beyond reactive pricing to strategic value creation.

The future of pricing is not a department – it is a way of thinking. For law firms, adopting it means not just adapting to the market, but helping shape the market on their own terms.

Implications for clients – becoming co-architects of value

The modernization of legal pricing cannot be achieved by law firms alone. While firms must evolve their systems, mindsets, and behaviors, so too must clients – especially in-house counsel, procurement teams, and legal operations. Too often, pricing reform is seen as a one-sided responsibility, with law firms expected to innovate while clients remain wedded to traditional behaviors and metrics.

If pricing is to become a source of mutual value rather than recurring friction, clients must embrace a more collaborative, commercially fluent, and strategically mature role. They must become co-architects of value.

From blunt cost control to strategic value

In many client organizations, the legal procurement function remains narrowly focused on bottom-line savings. Their success is often measured through metrics like year-on-year rate reductions, panel consolidation, increasing "value-adds" (freebies), or supplier negotiation leverage.

While understandable, these metrics are misaligned with the realities of legal work where complexity, risk, and outcomes vary greatly. A procurement model optimized for widgets struggles when applied to nuance, ambiguity, and advisory relationships.

This misalignment creates serious distortions. It encourages over-discounting, undervalues innovation, penalizes firms that invest in long-term improvement, and drives pricing models that may be cheap but unsustainable. Ultimately, it undermines trust and creates adversarial dynamics that are the antithesis of partnership.

To fully benefit from modern pricing models, clients must shift the focus from unit cost to total value. This means assessing legal spend through lenses such as:

- *Effectiveness.* Did the solution achieve the desired business outcome?

- *Efficiency.* Was the solution delivered in a cost-conscious, streamlined way?
- *Sustainability.* Is the pricing model viable for both sides over time?
- *Predictability.* Were expectations met, and were surprises avoided?

Procurement functions must evolve accordingly, developing the commercial fluency, data maturity, and incentive structures needed to support this more sophisticated approach.

Revisiting procurement incentives and KPIs

Just as law firms must revisit their meritocracy, compensation, and incentive structures, so too must client organizations and procurement in particular. Currently, many procurement professionals are bonused, evaluated, and promoted based on simple savings metrics. Success is defined by cost avoidance or percentage savings from "rack rates", irrespective of whether the resulting fee model is aligned with business needs or legal complexity.

This creates a powerful and often invisible barrier to progress. Even when in-house counsel or legal operations teams are open to more strategic models such as fixed fees, outcome-based pricing, or phased value delivery, procurement may resist, because those models don't easily fit legacy savings metrics. The result is a well-intentioned internal misalignment that sabotages innovation before it begins.

To correct this, procurement KPIs must evolve. A future-fit model would reward procurement teams not just for reducing cost, but for:

- Enabling value-for-money outcomes.
- Encouraging pricing model innovation.
- Supporting long-term supplier performance.
- Collaborating effectively with internal legal stakeholders and external partners.
- Delivering predictability, risk alignment, and efficiency gains.

In short, procurement must move from being cost controllers to value enablers. That shift will require leadership endorsement, metric redesign, and a cultural repositioning of procurement as a strategic partner to both legal teams and law firms.

Legal operations as translators and enablers

Legal operations functions are uniquely placed to bridge the gap between

176

procurement's commercial discipline and legal's service delivery requirements. To do so, they must also evolve, developing pricing fluency, data interpretation skills, and process design capability. The best legal ops teams are no longer just workflow engineers – they are value architects, capable of shaping how legal work is commissioned, priced, delivered, and evaluated.

This includes:

- Building internal pricing playbooks to guide negotiations and engagement with firms.
- Analyzing historical matter data to establish benchmarks and cost-to-serve patterns.
- Facilitating structured pricing pilots and feedback loops.
- Defining success metrics that go beyond spend reduction and towards business impact.

By becoming active co-creators in the pricing process, legal ops teams can ensure that pricing innovation is internally supported, operationally embedded, and strategically aligned.

Enabling transparent, two-way collaboration

Ultimately, the most important role clients can play is to create an environment where honest, open pricing conversations are not just tolerated but welcomed. This means being transparent about internal constraints (budgets, timeframes, risk appetites), business objectives (what good looks like), and priorities (speed vs depth, precision vs practicality).

It also means giving firms permission to explain pricing logic, offer alternative models, and propose trade-offs without fear of being automatically penalized. Firms often hold back because they fear that any deviation from standard fee formats will be misunderstood or rejected.

Clients can shift this dynamic by explicitly inviting innovation (and genuinely mean it), asking better commercial questions, and rewarding firms that propose smart, aligned solutions, even if they cost more than the lowest bidder. That kind of environment enables smarter scoping, more flexible structuring, and fewer pricing disputes.

In summary

Just as law firms must modernize their commercial approach, clients must rethink how they define, measure, and reward pricing success. Misaligned incentives – on both sides – are the single biggest obstacle to sustainable progress. Without reforming procurement KPIs, enabling legal ops to act strategically, and inviting firms to innovate without penalty, even the most advanced pricing models will remain underused and undervalued.

The most forward-thinking clients will recognize that pricing is not a one-time quote. It's a core mechanism for relationship health, value delivery, and mutual success. Those who step into that role will gain access to better solutions, stronger partnerships, and greater return on legal investment.

The human element – mindsets, habits, and resistance

No matter how powerful the pricing strategy, platform, or playbook, its success depends on human adoption. Yet the biggest obstacle to progress is not technical or structural, it's behavioral. Lawyers' mindsets, habits, and cultural conditioning continue to exert immense gravitational pull, often undermining even the most well-intentioned pricing reforms.

At the heart of this challenge lies a question the profession must now confront directly: *"How do we help lawyers become not just better practitioners, but more commercially fluent professionals – in a way that reflects the realities of how they work?"*

The traditional answers – classroom training, dense manuals, and one-off workshops – no longer suffice. Lawyers today are time-poor, task-saturated, and constantly context-shifting. They learn in fragmented intervals, often under pressure, and need insight in real time, and not just in theory. To shift pricing behaviors at scale, firms must embrace a new learning model – digital, personalized, and embedded in the flow of work.

Reimagining commercial capability building

The behavioral challenges around pricing – fear of financial conversations, resistance to fixed fees, aversion to scoping, discomfort with negotiation – are well known. But what's been missing is a learning architecture that meets lawyers where they are. The future of commercial capability-building must mirror how people actually learn now – on-demand, self-paced, modular, and supported by intelligent feedback loops.

Rather than expecting lawyers to attend infrequent day-long seminars, progressive firms will embrace:

- AI-enabled digital learning platforms with micro-learning modules on topics like scope setting, value communication, and pricing psychology.
- Bite-sized, scenario-based simulations that allow lawyers to practice pricing conversations, make decisions, and receive dynamic feedback.

- Self-guided learning paths that adapt to each lawyer's level of experience, practice area, and behavioral profile.
- Just-in-time support, such as chat-based pricing coaches, interactive templates, or embedded tooltips within pricing platforms.
- Mobile-first interfaces that allow lawyers to learn between meetings, on commutes, in a coffee break, or during brief windows of availability.

These tools don't just inform – they enable learning in context. They support confidence-building over time, provide immediate application relevance, and eliminate the disconnect between training and daily practice.

Shifting mindsets with smart nudges and embedded prompts

Lawyers don't resist pricing innovation because they're lazy or stubborn. They resist because pricing feels risky, ambiguous, and reputationally consequential. The solution is not just knowledge transfer – it's confidence scaffolding. Firms must create environments in which new behaviors are easier, safer, and more supported than the old ones.

Here, AI and automation have a major role to play. For example:

- When a partner creates a proposal in a program such as Virtual Pricing Director®, smart prompts highlight pricing risks or suggest alternative fee structures.
- If a lawyer selects a rate discount, the system might nudge them to justify the business rationale or model the margin impact.
- After a matter is completed, an AI assistant triggers a pricing debrief, offering insights into scope fidelity, write-offs, or profitability variance.
- When a pricing discussion is imminent, the lawyer might receive a short, tailored video on value framing or a quick checklist for client negotiation prep.

These interventions feel less like training and more like professional support tools. They create a subtle but powerful cultural shift – pricing becomes a topic lawyers engage with every day, not once a year.

Building psychological safety and commercial identity

Digital platforms and AI tools can do much, but they must be part of a broader ecosystem that fosters psychological safety. Lawyers need to feel safe experimenting with new pricing behaviors without fear of looking commercially naïve, losing face with colleagues, or risking client dissatisfaction.

Leaders and managers must set the tone – modelling openness, cultivating an environment in which constructive experimentation and even failure is not only tolerated but encouraged, celebrating small wins, and reframing pricing as a shared learning journey, not a performance test.

Crucially, the profession must reframe what it means to be a "great lawyer". That identity can no longer be defined solely by legal insight, technical brilliance, or rainmaking. It must include commercial fluency, pricing confidence, and value articulation. This evolution requires a shift in narrative – through peer storytelling, internal comms, and the elevation of those who demonstrate modern commercial acumen as role models.

Real-time support, not one-off events

One of the most valuable forms of learning is real-time coaching during live deals. Many firms are now embedding pricing professionals into matter teams – not just as approvers or reviewers, but as collaborative advisors. But even this model can be scaled through technology:

- An AI pricing assistant embedded in the firm's workflow could answer questions, suggest language, or highlight risks during proposal drafting.
- Proposal platforms could automatically populate fee structures from previous similar matters and surface lessons learned.
- Knowledge bots could answer, "How do I explain this scope change?" or "What's the margin impact of reducing our discount by five percent?"

These tools are not a substitute for human judgment – they are a multiplier. They create space for lawyers to learn by doing, with a safety net.

In summary

Transforming pricing behaviors requires transforming how lawyers are developed. It means shifting from episodic training to continuous enablement, from information-heavy lectures to embedded micro-learning, and from generic instruction to personalized, AI-driven support. It requires a culture that treats pricing not as a compliance task, but as a skill, a craft – one that can be learned, practiced, and mastered over time.

The future of commercial capability-building in law will not be classroom-led. It will be platform-powered, behaviorally intelligent, and aligned with the realities of how lawyers actually work. It will meet them in the flow of work – not in the back of a conference room. In doing so, it will empower a new generation of lawyers who see pricing not as a burden, but as a source of confidence, credibility, and client value.

From theory to practice – what progressive firms should do now

The case for pricing transformation is clear. The models are emerging. The tools are available. The client signals are increasingly unambiguous. But knowing *why* and *what* to change is only half the journey. The pressing question now is, how can progressive firms translate pricing ambition into everyday operational reality? This chapter provides a practical blueprint – grounded in commercial realism, not utopian design – for firms that are serious about moving forward.

Start by locating yourself on the horizon map

Every firm sits somewhere on the spectrum we've described – from Horizon one's overdue but manageable fixes, to Horizon two's cultural and structural rewiring, to Horizon three's bold experimentation. No firm can, or should, attempt to leap from traditional time-based pricing to autonomous AI-driven models overnight.

Instead, the key is to diagnose your current state honestly. Consider:

- Are you still overly reliant on ad hoc pricing led by individual partners?
- Do you have any meaningful fixed fee or alternative pricing models embedded?
- How often do you talk to clients about value – rather than just cost?
- Is pricing treated as a strategic issue in your leadership conversations?
- Do your lawyers have the tools, data, and support to price with confidence?
- Are you experimenting, learning, and iterating? Or stuck in defensive routines?

This self-assessment creates a shared baseline. It breaks the illusion that "We're doing fine" and instead surfaces specific gaps, contradictions, and opportunities. Firms that face these questions head-on unlock clarity of direction – a prerequisite for any lasting change.

Embed a lightweight pricing playbook

Firms don't need 100-page manuals to improve pricing discipline. What they need is a short, accessible, actionable playbook – designed not for compliance, but for empowerment. A good pricing playbook might include:

- Scoping checklists and common pitfalls.
- Sample assumptions and exclusions by matter type.
- Default fee model options with pros, cons, and margin guidance.
- Guidance on when and how to use fixed, capped, or retainer models.
- A shared vocabulary around value, risk, and price sensitivity.
- Advice on dealing with client pushback, scope creep, or mid-matter change requests.

The best playbooks live inside platforms, not in PDFs. They show up when lawyers need them, not when they're in "training mode". They evolve continuously based on firm experience – not just pricing theory.

Pilot and learn – don't wait for perfection
Transformation doesn't require perfection. In fact, perfectionism is the enemy of progress. Instead of waiting for firm-wide pricing overhauls, progressive firms start with pilots. They pick a team, client, matter type, or jurisdiction and trial something new – a fixed-fee structure with structured scope reviews, a technology-led proposal approach, a different KPI for evaluating profitability, or a pricing debrief model after deal closure.

Pilots work because they generate:
- Fast feedback loops.
- Visible results that build momentum.
- Internal case studies for broader buy-in.
- Safe environments for lawyers to experiment with new behaviors.

Critically, firms must measure what matters. Not just revenue or fee recovery, but margin performance, scope fidelity, client satisfaction, and lawyer confidence.

Train in the flow of work, not in isolation
As outlined in the previous section, firms must move away from event-based training and towards continuous enablement. This means:
- Micro-learning modules embedded in the tools lawyers use.
- AI-assisted coaching during proposal creation.
- Pricing nudges and prompts based on real-time decisions.
- Peer learning through pricing roundtables, retrospectives, or deal reviews.

Make pricing a weekly conversation, not an annual workshop. Celebrate the wins, share the learnings, and normalize the discomfort. That's how new behaviors take root.

Redesign the KPIs and conversations that shape behavior
If partners are still being measured solely on billings or utilization, pricing innovation will be a hard sell. To support change, firms must:
- Incorporate pricing quality, margin discipline, and scoping fidelity into performance conversations.
- Reward effort invested in pricing pilots, client co-design, or mentoring others.
- Recognize the commercial value of "not discounting" or walking away from unprofitable work.

This doesn't require a wholesale revolution of the comp model (yet) – but it does require alignment between what's said and what's measured. Senior leadership must talk openly about pricing, not just in strategy decks, but in boardrooms, town halls, and practice group meetings. Visible prioritization drives cultural signaling.

Involve clients in the journey
Progressive firms don't just impose new models – they co-create them with clients. That means:
- Inviting clients to test alternative fee structures.
- Running pricing retrospectives together.
- Asking what value really means in their context.
- Being transparent about risks, assumptions, and expectations.

This builds trust, strengthens relationships, and opens the door to deeper, more sustainable commercial partnerships. Clients want predictability, fairness, and alignment – not the lowest price. Firms that take the lead in shaping that conversation win more than just the work – they win loyalty.

In summary
Firms that want to lead in the next five years must do more than discuss pricing innovation – they must operationalize it, experiment with it, and embed it in the culture of how they work. That means:
- Assessing your current pricing maturity honestly.

- Equipping teams with smart, usable playbooks and digital tools.
- Supporting real-time learning and commercial confidence.
- Adjusting incentives and rewards to reinforce desired behaviors.
- Working *with* clients, not just quoting at them.

This isn't about achieving perfection overnight. It's about momentum, alignment, and intention. The firms that act now – pragmatically but boldly – will outpace those still waiting for the "right moment".

An optimistic future for those willing to lead

Pricing in legal services is no longer a footnote. It is a signal – of value, of strategy, of alignment. It is both a mirror and a lever. It reflects how firms think about clients, and it influences how clients think about firms. The next five years will test the legal profession's ability to adapt not just to economic pressure or technological disruption, but to a deeper truth – that how you price is as important as what you do.

This chapter has argued that pricing is the next frontier of competitive advantage, and not just in theory. The tools exist. The client appetite is growing. The commercial logic is overwhelming. Firms that grasp this moment will not simply optimize fees – they will redefine relationships, reputations, and results.

What's most encouraging is that the opportunity is not limited to the biggest or boldest firms. Pricing transformation is highly scalable. A mid-sized regional practice with the right mindset can outpace a global giant still tethered to legacy models. The future will reward clarity of intent, not just depth of resources.

To lead, firms must let go of outdated assumptions – that pricing is about time, that clients only care about cost, that lawyers can't talk about money, that value is too subjective to define. These are myths and they no longer serve us. The profession's future lies not in resisting change, but in embracing it with creativity, courage, and commercial empathy.

Yes, change is uncomfortable. Yes, it will require rewiring incentives, revisiting hierarchies, and retraining behaviors. But it is also energizing, empowering, and overdue. Pricing reform is not a burden. It is an invitation to be bolder. To speak more clearly about value. To build more resilient, rewarding partnerships. And to position legal services not as a reluctant cost, but as a confident, co-designed contributor to business success.

The next five years will be shaped by those firms that stop waiting, stop defending, and start designing. Those that reimagine pricing not as an administrative hurdle, but as a core part of their value story. Those that build cultures where commercial fluency sits alongside legal expertise – not as a rival, but as a complement. And those that see clients not as adversaries in price negotiations, but as collaborators in value creation.

The future is not set, but it is *available*. And it belongs to those willing to lead.

About Globe Law and Business

Globe Law and Business was established in 2005. From the very beginning, we set out to create legal books that are sufficiently high level to be of real use to the experienced professional, yet still accessible and easy to navigate. Most of our authors are drawn from Magic Circle and other top commercial firms, both in the United Kingdom and internationally. Our titles are carefully produced, with the utmost attention paid to editorial, design and production processes. We hope this results in high-quality publications that are easy to read and a pleasure to own.

In 2021, we were very pleased to announce the start of a new chapter for Globe Law and Business following the acquisition of law books under the imprint Ark Publishing. Our law firm management list is now significantly expanded with many well-known and loved Ark Publishing titles.

We are also pleased to announce the launch of our online content platform, Globe Law Online, which allows for easy access across firms. Details of all titles included can be found at www.globelawonline.com. Email glo@globelawandbusiness.com for further details and to arrange a free trial for you or your firm.

We'd very much like to hear from you with your thoughts and ideas for improving what we offer. Please do feel free to email me on sian@globelawandbusiness.com. Happy reading and thank you for your time.

Sian O'Neill
Managing director
Globe Law and Business
www.globelawandbusiness.com

www.ingramcontent.com/pod-product-compliance
Ingram Content Group UK Ltd.
Pitfield, Milton Keynes, MK11 3LW, UK
UKHW051840181025
464112UK00002B/28